EMPLOY-ABILITY PLUS

A Unique Plan to Assist the Job Seeker Who Can Accept a Challenge

By

Richard N. Diggs

My sincere thanks to all those who have supported my efforts to find and develop better job search instruction for the graduates of our post secondary schools. Special appreciation goes to my unique and loyal staff, my very knowledgeable and helpful sister Kathryn, my brilliant friend Bob Allen, and generous associates: John Benanti, John Cowan, Jim Kohl, George Hall, Bill Rodgers, Bill Goddard, Judith Harm, and Linda Hancock. And it goes without saying that much gratitude is overdue to my dear wife Shirley for her ongoing tolerance.

ISBN 0-937157-02-3

$6.95

Published by
Progressive Publications
P.O. Box 4016
Homosassa Springs, Florida 32647

Phone (904) 382-1452

FORWARD

Proper mental attitudes are powerful allies. They cost nothing, yet they are servants that work tirelessly on our behalf, forever producing positive results. They are the most influential factors in our lives.

There is much meaning, therefore, to the old adage "We are what we think about." If we think we can, then with a plan, we can. If we think we can't, no plan is necessary, we can't.

If we live with doubts and fears and allow them to exist, we have no recourse than to inhabit a self constructed dungeon.

If we sustain a positive attitude, our cheerfulness will lead to respect, self-confidence, accomplishment, and a very happy life.

Are we ordained at birth to be one way or the other? Definitely not! The choice is ours.

William James, the great psychologist, said: "The greatest discovery of my generation is that human beings can alter their lives by altering their attitudes of mind."

Unfortunately, far too many students, engulf themselves in negativism when contemplating the job they "would love to have."

They fail to realize that each of us is endowed with the inner-strength to exert a powerful influence over those we meet, . . . that our attitudes can be the contagious motivating factor that causes an employer to want our services.

In the pages that follow, we concentrate first on the formation of the proper mental attitude, . . . then on the actions, that as the result of positive thought, can enable you to get your "Ideal Job."

When you achieve the "right frame of mind" you will gain a sense of freedom you never have enjoyed before. You will not have to rely on others to give you a break, get you a job, and/or provide you with food to eat and a roof over your head. Your dreams and desires will not be tied to an inheritance, winning a lottery, schemes or chicanery.

Your attitude will be your security. And others will envy you for your wealth. Both for what you have acquired in dollars as well as your admirable integrity and the sincere admiration and love of all those who know you.

To assist you with your new attitude, which hopefully will be "I can" and "I will," we have included several poems and bits of wisdom throughout this book. If you ever begin to doubt your abilities, read them again. They will fortify your determination.

"The only limit to the realization of tomorrow will be our doubts of today."

Franklin Delano Roosevelt

TO THE YOUNG

THE great were once as you.
They whom men magnify to-day
Once groped and blundered on life's way,
Were fearful of themselves, and thought
By magic was men's greatness wrought.
They feared to try what they could do;
Yet Fame hath crowned with her success
The selfsame gifts that you possess.

The great were young as you,
Dreaming the very dreams you hold,
Longing yet fearing to be bold,
Doubting that they themselves possessed
The strength and skill for every test,
Uncertain of the truths they knew,
Not sure that they could stand to fate
With all the courage of the great.

Then came a day when they
Their first bold venture made,
Scorning to cry for aid.
They dared to stand to fight alone,
Took up the gauntlet life had thrown,
Charged full-front to the fray,
Mastered their fear of self, and then
Learned that our great men are but men.

Oh, Youth, go forth and do!
You, too, to fame may rise;
You can be strong and wise.
Stand up to life and play the man —
You can if you'll but think you can;
The great were once as you.
You envy them their proud success?
'Twas won with gifts that you possess.

Edgar A. Guest

HOW TO GET THE MOST OUT OF THIS BOOK

This book was not written to assist you to get "any old job." After all, you sure didn't need to go to school so you could be paid minimum wage or perhaps slightly higher. The sad fact is, however, that this may be what many of you will end up with if you don't reach higher. And you may not realize it, but a full time job at minimum wage still places you below the Poverty Line if you are trying to support anyone else in addition to yourself.

If you simply take the first job to come along, your chances of being satisfied are very slim. This will be increasingly more apparent as time goes by if you have chosen the wrong employer. Very often it takes years of broken promises and exaggerated excuses before you realize you have made a mistake.

Facts determined by national surveys bear this out!

- OVER 70% OF ALL U.S. WORKERS ARE NOT HAPPY WITH THEIR JOBS.
- THE MAJORITY OF U.S. WORKERS FEEL THEY ARE UNDERPAID FOR THE JOB THEY DO.
- THE MAJORITY OF U.S. WORKERS FEEL THAT THEIR BOSSES DON'T APPRECIATE THEM, DON'T WANT THEIR OPINIONS, AND NEVER COMPLIMENT THEM FOR WORK DONE WELL.
- THE MAJORITY OF U.S. WORKERS FEEL THAT OPPORTUNITIES FOR ADVANCEMENT DO NOT EXIST.

Most probably these are the reasons that the following statistic has been revealed:

- THE AVERAGE U.S. EMPLOYEE WORKS AT A PACE EQUAL TO 40% OF HIS OR HER PRODUCTIVE CAPACITY.

This being so, we can assume that the average U.S. company is going to have difficulty competing in the world marketplace. Fortunately, many more companies are waking up to the value of management techniques that allow for individual expression, recognition, rewards, and healthy employee morale.

Your challenge, as a job seeker, is to find these better employers, assuming you want to put 100% effort into your work in return for comparable monetary rewards, self satisfaction and happiness.

ONLY BY FINDING YOUR IDEAL EMPLOYER CAN YOU FIND YOUR *"IDEAL JOB"*

HERE'S OUR DEFINITION OF THE *"IDEAL JOB"*

- GOOD PAY.
- GOOD BENEFITS.
- THE OPPORTUNITY TO ADVANCE IN PAY AND POSITION IN RETURN FOR YOUR EFFORT AND EFFICIENCY.
- MANAGEMENT THAT ALLOWS AND ENCOURAGES THEIR EMPLOYEES TO THINK AND EXPRESS THEIR IDEAS AND OPINIONS.

- OWNERSHIP THAT CARES FOR THEIR EMPLOYEES AND SHOWS APPRECIATION FOR WORK WELL DONE.
- A FRIENDLY WORKING ENVIRONMENT.
- OWNERSHIP AND MANAGEMENT THAT OFFER INCENTIVES, ASIDE FROM WAGES, THAT ENCOURAGE WORKERS TO BE AT THEIR PRODUCTIVE BEST.
- A PLACE WHERE YOU CAN MAINTAIN THAT WONDERFUL FEELING THAT YOU BELONG, . . . AS AN INTEGRAL MEMBER OF A WINNING TEAM.

Is it difficult to find such a job? Of course! But it is certainly not impossible. As a matter of fact we can say it is probable if you follow these directions:

1. READ THIS BOOK FROM COVER TO COVER, THEN COME BACK TO CHAPTER ONE AND START AGAIN, THIS TIME COMPLETING THE ASSIGNMENTS.
2. CHOOSE A CLASSMATE OR CLOSE FRIEND TO WORK WITH, WHO IS ALSO LOOKING FOR A JOB. MAKE ARRANGEMENTS TO MEET DAILY TO EXCHANGE IDEAS AND INFORMATION, AND PRACTICE INTERVIEWING.
3. CONTINUE TO SEARCH FOR PROSPECTIVE EMPLOYERS WHO MAY BE ABLE TO OFFER YOU YOUR "IDEAL JOB." WORK NO LESS THAN FORTY HOURS PER WEEK IN YOUR PURSUIT.
4. CONTINUE TO PERFORM YOUR RESEARCH ON EVERY PROSPECTIVE EMPLOYER SO NO MISTAKE WILL BE MADE WHEN YOU ACCEPT EMPLOYMENT.
5. PERSIST WITH YOUR PLAN UNTIL YOUR SPECIFIC GOAL IS REALIZED.

FOOD FOR THOUGHT

As you perform your research and determine those employers you would love to work for, you will also discover that they have considerably less employee turnover. This means fewer job openings and greater competition when they do occur. It also means you have to meet this challenge by continuing to prepare. Go back to school if need be to pick up or improve the skills in which you are weak. Continue to research the company, finding out every thing you can about their products, services, methods of operation, etc. And continue to study this book and practice interviewing. Even if it should take months, maybe years, don't give up. Establish a plan utilizing the formula in Chapter 2, then go for it! You won't fail.

TABLE OF CONTENTS

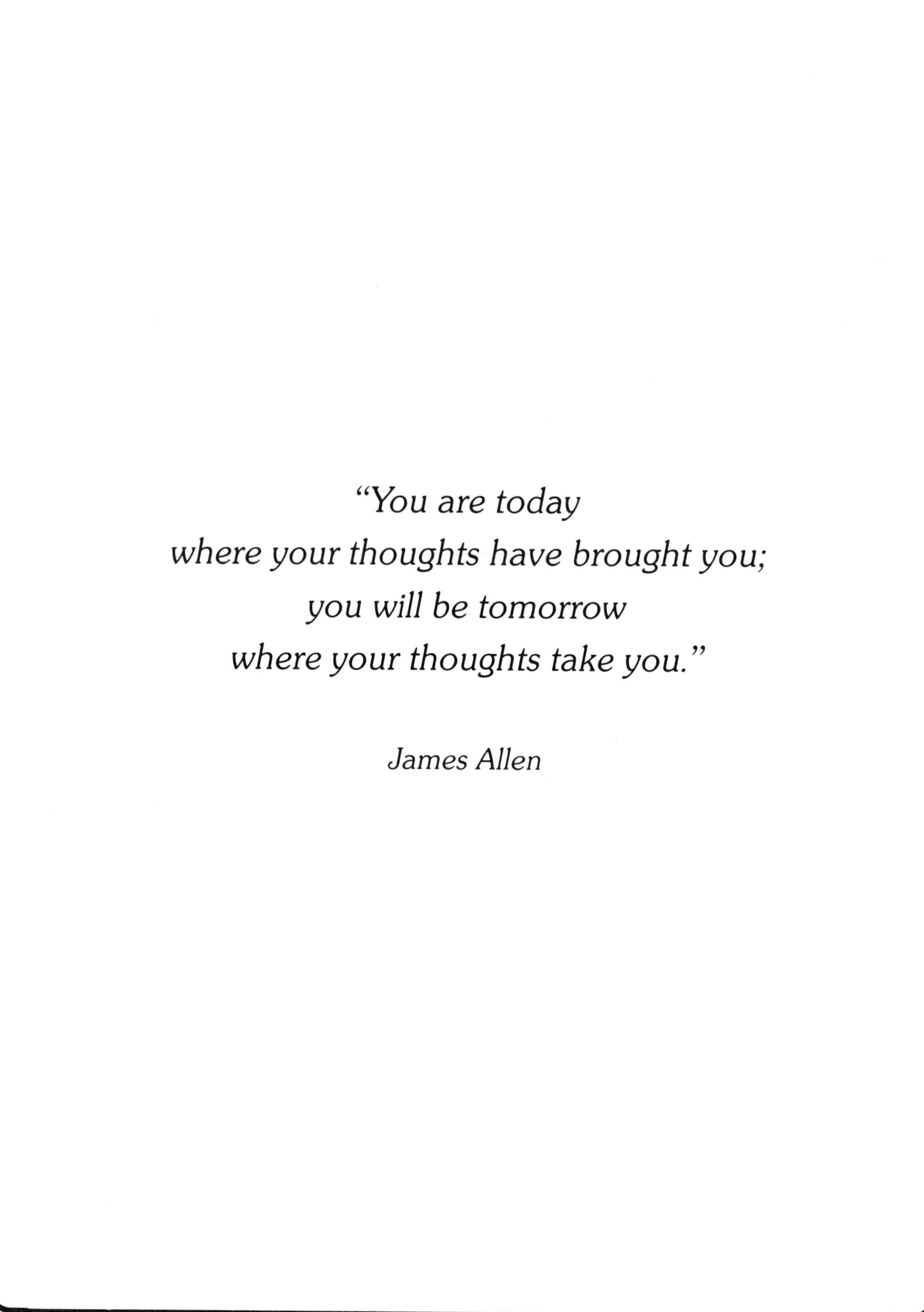

"You are today
where your thoughts have brought you;
you will be tomorrow
where your thoughts take you."

James Allen

CHAPTER 1

ABOUT YOUR MARKETPLACE

During the worst of times, there are people hired every day, in all kind of jobs, in all types of businesses. Even in a depression year, statistics show that no less than a million new jobs become available in the United States. A few million more openings are created by retirement, death, sickness, termination of poor workers, relocation, pregnancy, etc.

Why, then, are some people out of work for years? Simply put — because they haven't convinced any employer that the benefits they can offer are equivalent to the wage he or she must pay. These people either lack saleable skills or the ability to sell themselves in an interview.

Getting the job you want at the wage you feel you deserve is a skill in itself. Despite millions of jobs being available, there are also millions of people with whom you are competing. That's why the job search must be thoroughly planned. Luck seldom plays a role.

Luck is When Preparation Meets Opportunity.
Even a Four Leaf Clover Has No Significance to the Finder, If He Never Learned to Count.

Although it may come as bad news to learn that you will be competing with millions for a job, the good news is that less than one Job Seeker out of ten will do any preparation at all prior to showing up for an interview. So by the time you finish reading this book for the first time, you will just about eliminate 90% of your competition.

The other 10% will not be so easy to dispose of, but they, too, will fall by the wayside as you continue to strive to be the best that you can be. For as you increase both your occupational and job seeking skills, the law of supply and demand will become apparent.

There are always buyers for the rare and valued object. One-of-a-kind Jewels, Paintings, Automobiles, and even Bottles of Wine are constantly sold at ever increasing prices. The same is true of People. Wise employers are always in search of those "Hard-To-Find" workers who can make them money, save them money, or solve their problems.

If you are capable of showing and proving that you can satisfy an employer's desires, you will be forever in demand. And you will never have to settle for the low end of the pay scale for your profession. To do this effectively, you must assume the role of a salesman who is selling a very valuable product. This product is the only one of its kind in the entire world. This product can offer a multitude of unique benefits to anyone who possesses it. Sound easy to sell? We hope so, for the product is *YOU.*

Now if this thought has already created doubts in your mind, don't worry about it. We are going to help you create a plan that will erase your fears and boost you to a new level of self-confidence.

"A wise man
will make
more opportunities
than he finds."

Francis Bacon

CHAPTER 2

THE FORMULA FOR SUCCESS

Throughout the entire history of mankind, it has become apparent that those extraordinary men and women who are renowned for their accomplishments, all had something in common: A plan that included five major points. We pass them on to you here. Use them with all your might and you cannot fail. Only one prerequisite is necessary; your goal must be realistically believable.

"Anything the Mind Can Conceive, and Believe, Can be Achieved!"

If you intend to succeed at anything in your lifetime, you must have a plan. If you intend to find the "IDEAL" job, you must have a plan.

HERE ARE THE FIVE POINTS OF THE SUCCESS FORMULA

1. **ESTABLISH A BELIEVABLE GOAL. WRITE IT DOWN.**
   Be specific about the details of your plan and record the date when you intend to accomplish your goal. It is necessary to provide a "DEADLINE" for yourself.

2. **VISUALIZE YOURSELF ALREADY HAVING ACCOMPLISHED YOUR GOAL.**
   We become what we think about. Throughout each day, you must continually take the time to dream. The more you concentrate on what it will be like when your goal is realized, the more the details of your plan will fall into place. To keep this idea alive, we suggest you make a "THINGS I MUST DO TODAY" list every day from now on. Do this either at night before retiring, or the first thing in the morning. After you get in the habit of doing this, you will find that you will accomplish twice as much in the course of your working day.

3. **MAINTAIN A POSITIVE ATTITUDE.**
   We suggest three methods:
   A. Associate only with those who also are optimists. Rid your environment of those pessimists who constantly say "I CAN'T," or who tell you "YOU'LL NEVER DO IT." Share your dreams with your positive thinking friends.
   B. Use a concept which many have titled: "AUTOSUGGESTION." It is simply the procedure of repeating a positive statement over and over again. The mind is capable of amazing feats. Somehow it allows us to be what we think about if we continually make a statement. Muhammed Ali transformed himself into the Heavyweight Champion of the world by repeating "I AM THE GREATEST." Tom Monaghan brought his struggling Dominos Pizza Company to world prominence by saying "I AM GOING TO BE THE BEST PIZZA MAKER IN THE WORLD." Try it. It works.
   C. Take 15 minutes a day to read some self-improvement books. There are many of them on the market, but to get you started, try *The Power of Positive Thinking* by Norman Vincent Peale, or *Think and Grow Rich* by Napoleon Hill. They are two of the best and you shouldn't have any difficulty finding them at any library or bookstore.

4. **PERSEVERE. DON'T ALLOW YOURSELF TO GIVE UP.**
   Sure, you will encounter problems, but refuse to let them get you down. Have the courage to pick yourself up after every set-back, readjust your plan, and start again. Remember that failure is a great teacher, and that *"In every adversity, there is the equivalent of an equal or*

greater benefit." If you maintain this attitude you ultimately will succeed. Almost all failures that occur are the result of somebody giving up, or not being adequately prepared for the battle. Persevere.

5. **WORK-WORK-WORK-WORK-WORK.**
   You can't very well dream up clever ways to make a million, and then work a six hour day implementing your ideas. Nothing is that simple. If you want to succeed, forget about working average hours. There is a price to pay for success and it is an unrelenting, uncompromising, uncommon effort.

   This factor is very significant when it comes to finding the "IDEAL" job. Most Job Seekers are content to answer an ad or two and then sit home waiting for the phone to ring. They generally go long periods of time being unemployed, and then settle for the average job. The Job Hunter who puts in no less than 40 hours usually is quick to pick up his or her first paycheck. Procrastination can become a paralyzing illness. Work can be a tonic.

Use the form on the following page to organize your daily objectives. Make copies for at least a month in advance so you can schedule your follow-up appointments. Keep records on the back of these forms of all meetings and contacts. You must get in the habit of writing everything down. Keep all these forms in a 3-ring binder.

We have one more suggestion for you that will put more excitement and joy into every day. Make the first note on your "THINGS TO DO" list a humanitarian objective. A space is provided for this on the form. Simply put, this can be any act, deed, compliment, etc., performed in person or by phone, that makes it possible for someone else to have a great day because you cared. You'll feel terrific whether the recipient of your kindness is a relation, a friend, a stranger you see each day, or just someone you have read about who could use your help. Try it. Generosity has a way of going full circle.

THINGS I MUST DO TODAY. Day of the Week ________________ Date ____________

PHONE FOLLOW-UP

Person to talk to.	Position.	Name of company.	Phone No. and ext.

OTHER THINGS I MUST DO TODAY

1. ______________________________

2. ______________________________

3. ______________________________

4. ______________________________

5. ______________________________

6. ______________________________

7.

DAILY HUMANITARIAN OBJECTIVE

Today, I will help someone else have a great day! . . . I will ______________________________

RECORD THE OUTCOME OF EACH TASK HERE.

CHAPTER 3

SELF ANALYSIS

Before long, you will be sending cover letters to prospective employers in addition to your resume. Your purpose in doing so will be to interest someone in granting you an interview. To do this you must sell yourself in print. Likewise, when you get to the interview, you must sell yourself with words. When you are asked questions like: "What are your strong points?" or perhaps; "Tell me why I should hire you," you must be prepared.

This is not the time to be humble. After all, if you don't tell the interviewer about yourself, how is he or she to know you are worth the time of day. It is not considered "IN GOOD TASTE" to take your mother with you on the interview, so it is up to you to speak for yourself.

What do you say? What the employer wants to hear. For example, every employer is concerned about dishonesty. Millions are lost each year to employee theft. And almost every business is affected. Not only is money stolen, but enormous sums are lost due to pilfered supplies and equipment, fictitious expense accounts, phony sick days, and time spent goofing off when employees are supposed to be working. Internal theft, therefore, is a much greater problem than consumer theft. It is smart to tell the interviewer that you are honest. To sell this idea convincingly, however, just saying "I am honest" is not enough. You must follow up on your first statement with a second that makes the first believable, such as: "My parents instilled a conscience in me that is inflexible, consequently, I can't stand people who steal."

Here are a few more examples:

I make good use of my time . . . I took a class in time management a few years ago, and now feel I accomplish much more each day.

I know English well . . . Thanks to a very large Nun with a big stick.

I have always prided myself on being a hard worker . . . Dad got me a paper route when I was eight years old, and I've always had one or two jobs ever since.

I am always punctual . . . I have always felt that people who constantly show up late are rather inconsiderate.

OK, got the idea? Now here's your assignment. In the left hand column you will find a list of attributes that the average employer would like to find in every applicant. Circle only those that you honestly feel you possess in strong measure. Then in the right hand column write out a statement in your own words that makes that subject believable. By no means feel you must circle every topic. This exercise is to divulge your strong points so you can sell yourself with pride. It is not an exercise in creative writing.

EVERY EMPLOYER WANTS AN EMPLOYEE WHO	BACK-UP STATEMENT
Smiles frequently	______________________________
	______________________________
Has a sense of humor	______________________________
	______________________________

EVERY EMPLOYER WANTS AN EMPLOYEE WHO	BACK-UP STATEMENT
Has common sense	
Is not moody	
Is self-confident	
Is considerate of others	
Is well liked	
Is responsible	
Is ambitious	
Is honest	
Is well organized	
Is not a chronic complainer	
Is a positive thinker	
Is a hard worker	
Is patient with others	
Is in control of his temper	
Is humble	
Is efficient	
Is adept at handling people	
Is capable of self-discipline	
Is not inclined to argue	
Is not inclined to procrastinate	
Is inclined to plan ahead	

EVERY EMPLOYER WANTS AN EMPLOYEE WHO	BACK-UP STATEMENT
Can accept constructive criticism	________________
	________________
Can lose or make a mistake	________________
without excuses	________________
Can convey ideas clearly.............	________________
	________________
Can keep information told in	________________
confidence.......................	________________
Can refrain from slandering others ...	________________
	________________
Can speak and write English well	________________
	________________
Can listen carefully to directions	________________
	________________
Can praise the work of others	________________
	________________
Can complete a project on time.......	________________
	________________
Can persist when the going gets	________________
tough	________________

Armed with the answers you have just provided for yourself, you should be able to construct a strong case to present to any employer, giving sound reasons why you should be hired. To make your petition even stronger, though, make a list below of all the skills you have learned, both in school and through experience.

MY SPECIFIC SKILLS ARE:

____

____

____

____

____

____

____

____

____

____

____

NOW WE WILL DETERMINE THE WAGE YOU ARE GOING TO ASK FOR, BASED ON AVERAGE WAGES FOR THOSE IN THE POSITION YOU SEEK, AND A COMPARISON OF YOUR SKILLS AND ATTRIBUTES.

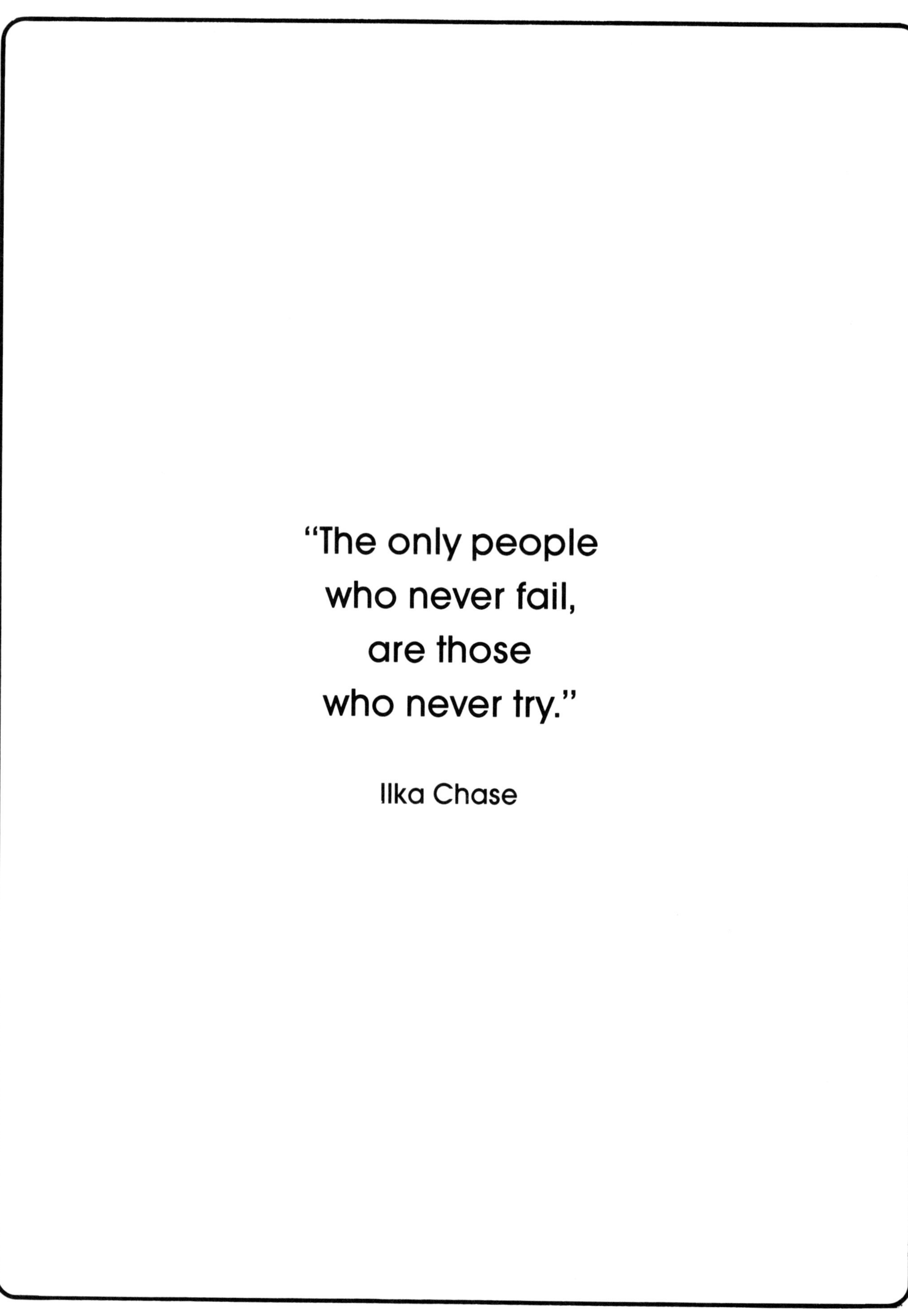

"The only people
who never fail,
are those
who never try."

Ilka Chase

CHAPTER 4

DETERMINING YOUR OWN WAGES

After assessing all of the benefits you have to offer an employer, and after determining a primary position you are going to work hard to get, it is time to put a price tag on this valuable, one-of-a-kind product.

Whatever you do, don't start out your job hunt with the idea, "I'll take anything." If your intention is to stay and advance in your career, then you must be fussy.

Perhaps you've seen this sign prominently displayed in many retail establishments:

"WE HAVE NO ARGUMENT WITH THOSE WHO SELL FOR LESS.
THEY KNOW WHAT THEIR PRODUCTS ARE WORTH."

If you tell prospective employers you'll work for less, you are telling them that you aren't worth more. Now, in so doing, you may get the job, but consider what you have given up — perhaps $2,500 in starting salary which you'll never retrieve! Over a working lifetime of forty years, we are talking about sacrificing $100,000 plus interest!

YOU MUST REMEMBER THIS POINT: WHETHER YOU GO TO WORK FOR AN EMPLOYER OR NOT IS AS MUCH YOUR DECISION AS IT IS THAT OF THE EMPLOYER.

That is why you must establish in your mind the salary and benefits you sincerely feel you are worth, and be firm and assertive with your request.

HOW TO ESTABLISH THE PRICE FOR YOUR SERVICES

First, go to your favorite Library and ask for the most current copy of the *Occupational Outlook Handbook*. This book is published annually by the U.S. Department of Labor. It includes information on just about every occupation, . . . work performed, average earnings, future demand, etc. Read all the data on the occupation you intend to go into, then answer the questions that follow on the next page.

Let's make a hypothetical example. The average secretary in the U.S. makes $18,577.00 per year, or $357.25 per week, plus medical insurance and a few other benefits (depending on the company). She has six (6) years experience, types at 55 wpm, and takes shorthand at 120 wpm. She knows how to use three (3) business machines, and one half of all secretaries in the country now know word processing.

If you were aspiring to get a secretarial position, you would then ask yourself these questions:

Do my skills match, or exceed, those of the average?

Does the experience I have match, or exceed, the average?

What unique qualifications do I have that will allow me to sell myself for a higher wage?

Do the wages in my geographic area match those of the national average?

What is the current demand for secretaries in my area?

Let's take another example: Electrical and Electronic Technicians.

Because this field is so broad, most Technicians specialize in one area, such as Research and Design, Manufacturing, Sales, or Customer Service. Employment in this field is expected to increase much faster than the average for all occupations through the 1990's. (This tells you that you have a much better chance of getting both the job and the wage you desire.) Latest statistics show the average technician earning an annual salary of $21,800.00. Those hired by the Government at entry level averaged about $12,800.00. Education and experience for specific job openings will determine starting wages.

So to determine the wage you intend to ask for, you must first narrow your goal so you can relate your education, experience, and personality characteristics to a very specific position. When you have done this, we then suggest that you go to prospective places of employment and talk to those who are working in similar jobs to those you would like to have.

Unlike the Secretarial example, you must do considerably more research before filling in the answers that follow here.

If your training and experience has prepared you for a wide variety of opportunities, you, too, must make many more calls and visits.

Do your homework here:

Job Being Sought: ____

____

What are the skills and qualifications of the average worker in this occupation? ________

____

____

Average Earnings: ____

____

What are my skills and qualifications as compared to the average worker in this occupation?

____

____

____

____

____

I sincerely feel that I am worth $____________ in annual salary; consequently, I will place my request for wages in the range of $ ____________ to $ ____________.

This formula will work with most occupations and, in particular, for those where demand equals or exceeds supply.

THE EXCEPTION

There are times, however, after you have exhausted every means, when you might as well forget about holding out for a given wage. If you are attempting to break into a field that is highly desirable, occupied by few, and/or where supply far exceeds demand, you have two options: Go into another field of endeavor or concentrate on simply getting your foot in the door. Swallow your pride. Forget that you have a diploma or a college degree. Start in the mailroom if you can. As a matter of fact, if the position you seek is one you have always dreamed about having, offer to work for nothing. Just make sure the employer is the type you would care to work for, year after year; one who will reward ambition and effort.

This, of course, can be accomplished, but be aware that, to avoid spending countless hours in a dead end pursuit, your research must be thorough. Count on spending at least twice the time it would take you to examine your prospective employers as it would take if you were applying for a garden variety position.

NOW LET'S PROCEED TO FIND THAT IDEAL EMPLOYER.

"As long as we
have not given ourselves
reason to trust our abilities,
we can but
plead for luck."

Arendee

CHAPTER 5

FINDING PROSPECTIVE EMPLOYERS

When we shop for a new car it is wise to go to many dealerships and compare. It is important to know the benefits that each make and model has to offer. It is also significant to evaluate prices, guarantees, service, future resale value, options, estimated mileage, etc. Most of us are smart enough to do this. After all, a few days well spent, could save us a thousand dollars or so.

When it comes to getting a job, however, most all of us turn downright stupid. Here is a decision that involves hundreds of thousands of dollars over the period of our working lifetime and most of us treat it as casually as if we were buying a pack of gum.

Some stranger says: "We'll pay you X amount," and based on that alone, millions of us each year report for work.

It is no wonder that over 70% of all American workers say they are not happy with their jobs.

Certainly, money is foremost in our mind when we are looking for a job; but if we must put in eight or nine hours a day working for a tyrant, with co-workers who aren't mentally or emotionally compatible, with duties which aren't a challenge (or which are too much of a challenge), etc., we may conclude that the wage is not worth the trauma of coming to work.

So, finding the ideal job for you is not simply finding an employer who will say, "Yes." To be happily employed, you, too, must say; "Yes, this is the place I want to work."

Hopefully, you now realize that shopping for a job is perhaps the most momentous challenge you have ever been presented with. Think about this: This decision involves the commitment of about one third of all the hours you have to spend on this earth.

The more prospective employers you examine, the better your chances are of finding your "Ideal Job." The careful shopper has a much greater opportunity of making an intelligent decision.

We have prepared a form to assist you with your shopping. It appears on the next page. It is titled, "The Prospective Employer Information and Follow-Up Form." Take this book to a copy machine and make no less than 15 copies of this form (both sides). Then put them in the 3-ring binder along with the "Things I Must Do Today" forms which you made earlier.

This form includes basic data on the top of the front side, then space to do your in-depth research, then room to record follow-up on the back. Take a look at this form now so you can understand what we are talking about.

We will cover the in-depth research and follow-up later. Right now, your assignment is to find out the basic information on Employers who just might be able to offer you your "Ideal Job." Don't concern yourself with whether they are hiring now or not. The important thing right now is finding every employer you can find, through any source, that might fulfill your desires. If you can find more than 15, by all means do it.

PROSPECTIVE EMPLOYER INFORMATION AND FOLLOW-UP FORM

____
DATE

Name of Company ____________________ Founded __________

Address ____________________ Zip Code __________

Phone ____________________ No. of Employees (Approximate) __________

Products or Services ____________________

Source of Lead — Name ____________________ Position __________

Phone ____________________ If newspaper ad — glue to page.

RESEARCH ON THIS COMPANY

Name of Hiring Official ____________________ Phone __________ (Ext.)

Receptionist's Name ____________________ Name of Secretary __________

What employees at this company feel about the hiring official (personality, hobbies, character, what characteristics are significant, family, car driven, etc.): ____________________

How does the hiring official dress? ____________________

Do employees of this company like working there? (Record comments) ____________________

Does this company subscribe to equal employment opportunities? ____________________

What is the company record on promoting minorities? ____________________

Are there women in management positions? __________ Blacks? __________

Is the company profitable? Growing? Competitive? ____________________

Benefits offered: ____________________

Does the company promote from within? ____________________

Does the company believe in merit raises? ____________________

What problems might the hiring official consider to be of priority to solve? ____________________

____

What is the % of employee turnover? ____________________

If you determine a firm is in trouble, drop the idea of going to work there. Here are five (5) danger signs of pending collapse:

1. Have profits declined steadily over the past two years in successive quarters? __________
2. Has the stock value declined over the last four years? __________
   Note comparison from __________ to __________.
3. Have they had recent failures with new products and/or services? __________
4. Has the firm recently changed banks? ______ Treasurers? ______
   Accountants? ______ Advertising agencies? ______ Marketing strategies? ______
5. Have benefits been trimmed? ______ Budgets significantly cut? ______
   Research eliminated? ______

RECORD OF FOLLOW-UP

Date resume, cover letter, and materials sent: ____________________

Date of phone follow-up mentioned in cover letter: ____________________

Results of phone follow-up: ____________________

____

Interview set for (Date): __________ (Time): __________

How you felt the interview went (note your feelings and what you felt, afterward, that you could have done differently): ____________________

____

____

Thank you letter sent (Date): ____________________

Date for follow-up mentioned in thank you letter: ____________________

Result of follow-up phone call: ____________________

____

FINDING PROSPECTIVE EMPLOYERS

Explore every one of the following methods. You cannot afford to overlook any source when searching for your "Ideal Job." Work them simultaneously.. Fill out the top portion of a "Prospective Employer Information" sheet each time you develop a new lead.

1. SCHOOL PLACEMENT DEPARTMENTS

If you are working with a school placement department, you must realize that it is not their responsibility to get you a job. You should further realize that just because the school gives you a lead on a job order, or makes it known that interviewers from specific companies are scheduled on campus, there is no assurance that the jobs or the employers are worth their salt.

When you do get a lead from your school, fill out one of the "PROSPECTIVE EMPLOYER INFORMATION FORMS." It is vitally important that you perform research on every potential employer before being interviewed.

2. EMPLOYMENT AGENCIES

YOU PROBABLY WILL GO THROUGH AT LEAST TWO INTERVIEWS, IF YOU GO TO AN AGENCY. IS IT WORTHWHILE?

You betcha! Many fine corporations use agencies and executive search firms to find the employees they want. Running ads in newspapers, and parading through thousands of resumes and numerous interviews, are not only very costly undertakings for a company, but often risky ones. In this day and age of civil rights expression, many applicants who have been turned down for employment will take the matter to court, alleging any number of infractions in the hiring practice.

These lawsuits are expensive for companies, regardless if there are any well-based grounds for the suit. So, although they pay an agency for screening applicants, they may end up paying considerably less than if they ran their own ads.

Estimates vary, but it is safe to say at least 75% of all job offerings never appear in the newspaper or on TV or radio.

CONTACT EMPLOYMENT AGENCIES WHERE THE EMPLOYERS PAY THE FEES.

This information is available to you by checking the display ads in the Yellow Pages under "Employment Agencies" and under newspaper classified ad columns of the same title.

Check these sources right now and record the information below.

NAME OF AGENCY	ADDRESS	PHONE

You will follow these up later when you get to Chapter 8.

WHAT ABOUT TEMPORARY HELP AGENCIES?

Many large corporations have now gone to a policy of using only temporary help agencies to fill all vacancies for lower and mid-level positions. I believe this trend will continue to grow for several very sound reasons. The company does not have the obligation to offer benefits or pay employee taxes, and if the worker does not perform up to the standards expected, they can be immediately replaced. Companies realize they no longer need to gamble when hiring. They can try any number of people on a given job until they find one that is superior. They can then offer this person full-time employment.

From the employer's standpoint it makes a great deal of sense. Are there any advantages for the employee? Definitely, but only for those who maintain the attitude that they will do their very best at each assignment. For only these people will ultimately be offered full-time employment with full benefits.

It is not a bad scheme for those right out of school who lack experience. It also provides an immediate income while you continue the pursuit of your "ideal" job.

Now write the names of temporary help agencies here:

NAME OF AGENCY	ADDRESS	PHONE

You will follow these up later when you get to Chapter 8.

All temporary help agencies will test your skills at no charge, so it is also a means to determine where you now stand if you have been absent from the job market for awhile. You will then have a pretty good idea if you have current marketable skills or if you will need to return to school for additional training.

These agencies earn their money by performing an elimination service for employers, recommending only those who, in their opinion, are qualified for specific jobs. You must, therefore, sell yourself to the agency in much the same way you would if you were in direct contact with the employer. For this reason, we recommend that you wait to call these agencies until after you have completed Step Five. When you are ready to call for interviews, you are also ready to make calls to these agencies.

3. CHAMBERS OF COMMERCE

Contact the Chamber of Commerce in each city you would like to work and request their membership catalog. Fill out a *Prospective Employer Information* form for each potential employer.

4. LIBRARIES

Go to your Public Library (or school library) and ask the head librarian for help. Librarians, for the most part, are very helpful people and enjoy finding solutions. There are many directories of specific types of businesses available. Fill out a *Prospective Employer Information* form for each employer that meets your criteria.

5. NEWSPAPERS

Consult the help wanted columns of your local newspapers. (Sunday issues are always your best bet.) Fill out *Prospective Employer Information* forms only for those employers who meet your criteria. It's a good idea to cut out the ad and glue it on the form. Avoid blind ads that just ask you to write to a P.O. Box or to a box at the newspaper, unless the qualifications and job description make you feel ideally suited.

6. YELLOW PAGES

The Yellow Pages is another source of potential employers. Look under "Trade Associations" for specific areas of interest, then call them to get a membership directory. Also, look under the category titles. Again, fill out the *Prospective Employer Information* forms for those places of employment that seem interesting.

7. STATE EMPLOYMENT SERVICES

Every state has a free employment service that works in cooperation with the U.S. Department of Labor. Although most people assume that few of the better jobs are referred to the state agency, some surprises do occur. Services include counseling, testing, and placement. You can usually locate the nearest office to your home by looking in the white pages under your state's government listings.

NAME OF AGENCY	ADDRESS	PHONE

You will follow these up later when you get to Chapter 8.

A word of advice — many people assume that, because they are going to a government agency, their appearance isn't important. Not so! If a counselor is to refer you to one of the better jobs, he must be completely sold on you. Impress this person and you have an agent who will take pride in recommending you. Show up looking like a refugee from a war-torn country, and the only referrals you'll get will be to those employers who would like to hire war-torn refugees (and that's so they can work your head off for meager wages).

Any time you go to talk with someone about a job, look and act your best.

8. FEDERAL JOB INFORMATION CENTERS

Every state has a Federal Employment Agency whose job it is to place applicants in Civil Service jobs working for the U.S. Government. Whereas they were formerly known as the Civil Service Commission, the current title of the department is the Office of Personnel Management.

Look for listings in the white pages of your phone book under U.S. Government. Find the sublistings under either Federal Job Information Center or Office of Personnel Management.

Call them and ask if they are accepting applications for the career you would like to pursue. If so, write the name, address, and phone number below.

NAME OF AGENCY ADDRESS PHONE

____

____

____

____

____

You will follow these up later when you get to Chapter 8.

You should also know that just because they are accepting applications for a specific job is no indication a job is available. After acceptance, you could spend a long period of time waiting for the phone to ring. This source is definitely worth investigating, however. Particularly if you hold security in high priority.

9. EVERYONE YOU MEET

Talk to everyone you meet about their job and place of employment. Find out if it's a good place to work, if they are progressive, promote from within, have good benefits, are hiring now, etc.! If you like what you hear, right then and there, get out paper and pencil and make notes. If you can get the name of the person who does the hiring, by all means, write it down.

This is, by far, the most effective method as it may lessen the necessity for further research — if you have time to ask all the right questions. If, for some reason, you don't have time, ask the person you are talking to if you may call them later for more details. If so, don't fail to get a phone number.

If you live a sheltered life, it is time you break out of your shell. Make a point of going to places where people might be who are working in the profession you would like to pursue.

a) Call City Convention Centers. Get a schedule of upcoming conventions, seminars, etc. Record the events and dates that interest you.

EVENT DATE

____

____

____

____

____

b) Get back to the library. Find the book titled, "*National Trade and Professional Associations of the United States and Canada and Labor Unions.*" It is published by Garrett Park Press, Garrett Park, Maryland 20766. Also, locate the *Encyclopedia of Associations* published by Gale Research, Book Tower, Detroit, Michigan 48226. Make a list of the associations comprised of people in your desired profession. Write them, asking for information on membership, local chapters, national meetings, conventions, seminars, etc. ______________________________

____

____

____

____

c) Watch your local newspapers and magazines for social events where you could meet people of your desired economic status. Jot them down.

EVENT DATE

____

____

____

____

____

d) Talk to the butcher, the baker, the candlestick maker or whomever you come in contact with each day. Simply say, "Do you know of anyone who would like the opportunity to hire the best bookkeeper (or whatever) in the world?" Really, any such light, personable question is OK. You'll be surprised how many lead referrals you will come up with! Write below the question you will use to solicit job openings.

____

____

____

For each lead you get by asking people questions, fill out another copy of the *Prospective Employer Information* form.

Now, if you've gone about this business of finding prospective employers seriously, you should have a great number of these forms partially filled out (less the follow-up information that has yet to be gathered).

You can realize, now, why we advocate no less than forty (40) hours a week be spent on your Job Search. Take heart, it will be time well spent.

YOU MUST NOW PROCEED TO FIND THE INFORMATION ON EACH PROSPECTIVE EMPLOYER WHICH YOU HAVE YET TO OBTAIN. WORK BY PHONE AND PERSONAL VISITS TO GET THIS INFORMATION.

"All that is valuable
in human society,
depends on the opportunity
for development
accorded
the individual."

Albert Einstein

CHAPTER 6

RESEARCHING PROSPECTIVE EMPLOYERS

THIS IS THE MOST IMPORTANT ASPECT OF YOUR JOB SEARCH. IF YOU AREN'T KNOWLEDGEABLE ABOUT THE POLICIES, PROCEDURES, AND ATTITUDES OF PROSPECTIVE EMPLOYERS, YOU ARE GAMBLING WITH YOUR OWN FUTURE. YOUR CHANCES OF FINDING YOUR *"IDEAL JOB"* ARE ONLY ENHANCED WITH AWARENESS.

Over the years I have worked with hundreds of students who were thrilled to announce that they "just got a great job." They could hardly contain their exuberance. Two weeks later they were back looking for help to find them another job. Their horror stories about their former employers varied widely, but one point became clear, they could have determined these problems in advance, had they done any research.

So do your homework! Find out all you can about every employer before you even waste your time setting up an interview.

WORK BOTH BY PHONE AND BY MAKING PERSONAL VISITS

If you are researching a small firm, with up to fifty employees, you can usually find out all you need to know over the phone.

HOW TO SELL YOURSELF OVER THE PHONE

Before you pick up the phone, put a smile on your face and keep it there. Phone lines can't hide frowns, despair, or anger, and neither can they believe the fact you are grinning from ear to ear. To make sure you don't forget this, invest in an inexpensive makeup mirror (if you don't have one), and set it up next to your phone.

It is easy to say "no" to a negative person whose tone of voice is unfriendly, or just plain boring. It is almost impossible to say "no" to an enthusiastic, sparkling, personable, smiling positive thinker.

If you have acquaintances or names of referred persons working for a prospective employer, then by all means call them first. If they don't know the answers to your questions, ask them to give you the name or names of others who might. It is always easier to contact a stranger when you can say, "So and so suggested I call you."

WHO DO YOU ASK FOR AT A COMPANY WHERE YOU DON'T KNOW ANYONE?

You might start with the receptionist. Be honest and sincere, in addition to having a smile in your voice. "Good morning, and I sure hope you can help me. I am interested in the field of ______________________ (or) I just graduated from ______________________ and I'm trying to find the best employer to work for. Could you please put me in touch with the friendliest person in your ______________________ department?"

If you are swiftly shuttled to the personnel department, get the person's name first, then his or her position, then proceed to say why you are calling. If they say, "Sorry, we aren't hiring anyone right now," respond with, "Oh, that's OK, the research I am doing now is to prepare myself to be ready when openings do occur. Could you just give me two minutes of your time?" Seldom will you receive a "no!"

Now, if you are saying to yourself, "I can't phone and just talk to people I never met before," get the thought out of your head. Yes you can! Pick up the phone with an "I've got absolutely nothing to lose" attitude and force yourself to call. If you smile and convey enthusiasm, you will be surprised at what you can accomplish.

Remember — the worst thing that can possibly happen to you is that someone will hang up! Keep reasoning with yourself. If need be, pick up a book on assertiveness and study it.

If you find that those you talk to are very cold, rude, and/or evasive, don't think you have wasted your time calling them. You have found out that good manners, training, and management are evidently lacking in this company, and as such, it would not be an enviable place to go to work.

THE PERSONAL VISIT

Particularly with larger companies, we suggest you take the time to make a personal visit if at all possible. You'll simply get a better feel of the place than you will ever be able to get over the phone. You can measure the distance to work, the availability of parking, security, the neighborhood, the care of the facilities, the morale of the staff, the efficiency of those who greet you, the size of the operation, the products and/or services provided, and much more. You'll also have a chance to ask everyone you meet that all-revealing question: "Just between you and I, is this a good place to work?"

If you start your visit by talking to a receptionist, phrase your first question in the same way we suggested as a telephone technique. Ask for help. Psychologically speaking, most people like to help others when approached humbly. Those in a position to respond are recognized as being important, and as such they want to show and tell what they know.

While conversing with people, don't be bashful about asking for brochures, printed policies and procedures, employee handbooks, annual reports, etc. All of these can be extraordinarily helpful when you are preparing your marketing materials and preparing for the interview.

HINT

While in conversation, ask if the company is hiring now and, if so, for what positions. If any of these sound like jobs you would care to have, and are qualified for, then ask, "Would it be possible to get a written job description of that position?"

If you are able to get a written job description, prior to applying for a job, you have a step up on every other applicant as you can tailor-make a resume to fit the requirements for the job.

RELOCATION

If you have been giving any serious thought to the possibility of starting a new life in a different location, then do it wisely. Plan ahead. Those that just pack-up and move, with the idea that they will find a job when they arrive, are often sadly disappointed.

ASK YOURSELF THESE QUESTIONS:

1. Is a person with my skills needed in this area?
2. Will I be able to find my "Ideal Job"?
3. Can I find adequate housing that is within my means?
4. How does the cost of living differ from where I am now?
5. What are the taxes like there as compared to where I am now?
6. Will shifts in the population adversely affect the future economy of this area?

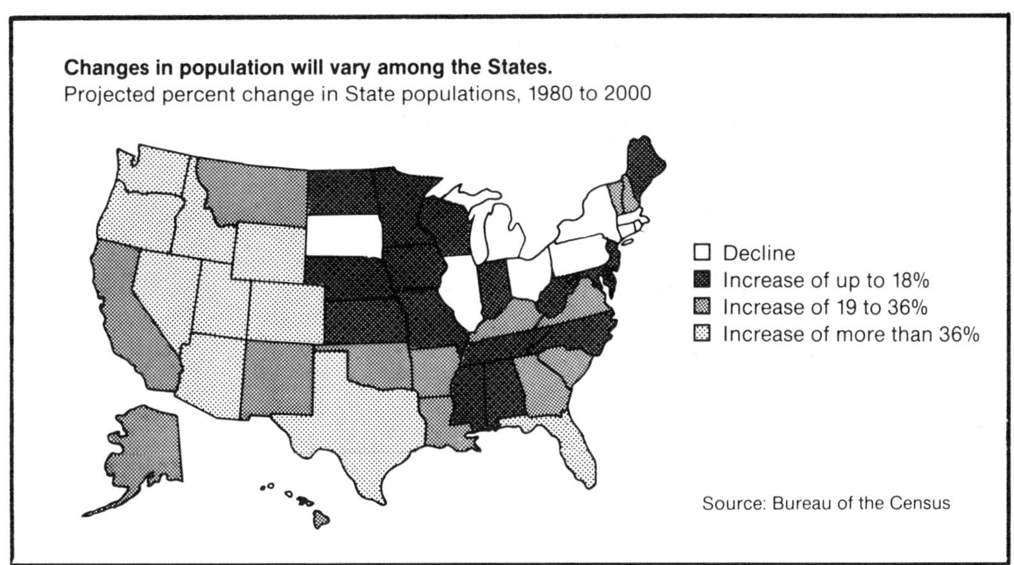

7. Can I adjust to new friends and new customs?
8. How much will I miss my friends and family?
9. Can I adjust to new weather conditions?
10. Are the means available to match the social and cultural activities that I favor?
11. How costly is the fare should I want to return home to visit?
12. What is it going to cost me to move?

If you don't know the answer to any of these questions, then start writing letters to anyone you know, the Chamber of Commerce, prospective employers etc. Then, if at all possible, go for a visit. Don't accept hearsay. Find out for yourself.

"I am only
an average man
but, by George,
I work harder at it
than the average man."

Theodore Roosevelt

CHAPTER 7

PREPARING RESUMES, LETTERS, ETC.

If you were a salesman, it is unlikely that you would set out to sell any product without collateral material to prove to your prospect that it is worthwhile for him to part with his money in exchange for the benefits the product has to offer.

Among these pieces of material might be:

A) A calling card or letter of introduction. (A cover letter to be sent with other materials, if you are the product.)

B) A brochure on the usefulness and versatility of the product based on the verifiable experience of others. (Your resume if the product is you.)

C) Brochures on the quality of the product (letters and articles attesting to your character, integrity and personality. If the product is you.)

D) A brochure on the service, company policies, and guarantees of the product. (Letters of reference from former employers if the product is you.)

Let's take these one by one. Keep in mind our materials must be professional looking, comprehensive yet brief and, first and foremost, selling tools.

Before proceeding any further, though, let's make one thing abundantly clear: despite what I state here as suggested procedure to follow, and despite what you might read in other job search books, magazines or newspapers, there is *not* simply a right way and a wrong way to write a cover letter, compose a resume or consider sending other materials.

If you want to group segments differently in your cover letters and resumes, be my guest. Do they sell? That's the only question you must keep asking yourself. If you feel a photograph would assist you to sell your story, go ahead and send it along. Whatever you do, just use common sense and good taste.

Now by saying good taste when referring to photographs, we don't mean just a snapshot of yourself because you feel you're plenty good looking. No. No. No, – what we are talking about are photos which tell a story. You and the sign in front of your own one person art exhibit, you and the proto-type car you built, you in front of a building you designed, you with landscaping you created, etc. The only time a picture of you alone might be appropriate is when the job obviously requires good looks, such as a model, a TV personality, a spokesperson, etc.

As an employer of many, I have looked at countless stereotyped cover letters and resumes, all of which appeared to have come off the same assembly line. It has often been a pleasant deviation to find the occasional person who knows how to put personality in print or who uses creativity to say, "Hey! Look at me! I'm not just the product of an education factory."

THE COVER LETTER

The cover letter is your introduction to a prospective employer. Its purpose, as with your other marketing materials, is to get the interview.

The cover letter should briefly state the reason you are writing, why you are interested in working for this company, and a request for an interview (or further contact).

Cover letters vary in structure. You will use one form to send to those employers whom you know are looking to hire an employee — quite another to the company you want to work for, who, to your knowledge, has not advertised for help.

Incidentally, do not send a hand-written letter. Have your letter typed, and be sure your grammar is perfect and your spelling is flawless. Never send a copy. This is an indication that you really don't care about this job. The recipient will quickly get the feeling that you've sent the same letter to many others, whether you have or not. Use white or light-colored bond paper, 8½x11. Most important, know the name and title of the person you are writing to and be positive the spelling of the name is correct. Letters to "To Whom It May Concern" or "Dear Sir" or "Madam" seldom reach the desired destination, and even when they do, they usually hit the wastebasket within minutes.

To sell effectively in these letters, we must include those assets we possess which can be of benefit to the employer. Consequently, it is now time to bring the skills and accomplishments you listed in Chapter 3 into play.

Go back to pages 15, 16 and 17 and relist here all the items you recorded. As you use them in your materials, check them off in the box at the right.

1. ______________________________ ☐
2. ______________________________ ☐
3. ______________________________ ☐
4. ______________________________ ☐
5. ______________________________ ☐
6. ______________________________ ☐
7. ______________________________ ☐
8. ______________________________ ☐
9. ______________________________ ☐
10. ______________________________ ☐
11. ______________________________ ☐
12. ______________________________ ☐

On the following pages are examples of cover letters, one for an advertised position, the other to a firm which you have determined to be "a good place to work."

This is an example of a cover letter you might send in response to an ad.

800 Main Street
Puma, Arizona 12345
(527) 825-1718

July 10, 19--

Ms. Jane Jones
XYZ Company
Los Angeles, California 90015

Dear Ms. Jones:

Having spent 14 years in school, getting more serious with each succeeding year, I am now ready for a career. While being educated, I simultaneously held three challenging secretarial jobs which required alert, responsible action and superior clerical skills. I feel I am now a finished product — personable, reliable, efficient and fun to be around.

Your ad in The Sunday News, which appeared July 9, sounds like the position I have long been preparing to find. I am enthusiastically interested. My resume is enclosed.

If my qualifications appear to suit your company's needs, I would like very much to establish a time for an interview. My telephone number is (527) 825-1718. I will follow up with a phone call within a week. I look forward to meeting you.

Sincerely,

Stacey Austin

Enclosure

This is an example of a cover letter which might be sent to a company that, to your knowledge, has not advertised for help.

July 10, 19--

Ms. Jane Jones
XYZ Company
Los Angeles, California 90015

Dear Ms. Jones:

In an attempt to find a company with which I might spend a working lifetime, I have searched, researched and soul-searched while narrowing my list.

I have found no others to compare with the XYZ Company. Consequently, I would very much appreciate the opportunity to be considered for a position with your firm.

Throughout my years of endeavor, which began at the age of eight, I have learned the value of integrity, the efficiency which comes as the result of self discipline, the pride of influencing, managing and working with others and the great joys of giving.

I believe, as an employee, I set an example through just plain old-fashioned hard work and yet I'm good natured and fun to be around.

My resume and other materials are enclosed. Please consider them in view of openings which may occur.

I'm very serious about my desire to work for your company. Consequently, I will be calling you on Friday, July 14, to discuss the possibility of an interview.

Should you care to contact me prior to receiving my call, my telephone number is (527) 825-1718.

Sincerely,

Stacey Austin

Now, draft a letter you might send in response to an ad which sounds interesting to you. Choose one out of the want ads and glue it in the space below.

GLUE AD HERE

Now, draft another letter which you might send to a company where you would like to work. Include as many benefits as you can from the list you have made on page 38.

THE RESUME

As large companies receive as many as 250,000 resumes a year, it is easy to understand that the vast majority make their way to the garbage pickup area within hours of the time the mailman makes his rounds.

Here is a list of "do's" and "don't's" worth considering:

1. Keep the resume on one page if at all possible, but don't sell yourself short. Use two to three pages if necessary, as long as it is as concise as possible.
2. Avoid "bold" or "fancy" paper. Use 8½x11 bond paper. White, light blue, light gray, buff and ivory are acceptable. No dark paper.
3. Be specific, choosing active verbs that better illustrate your activities. For example, "Worked on Muscular Dystrophy Fund Drive" might better read, "Originated, organized and coordinated a very successful MD walkathon, raising $37,000 for Jerry's Kids."

   Other words worth utilizing: created, developed, responsible, succeeded, expanded, implemented, established, completed, achieved, planned, conceived, expedited, managed, supervised, demonstrated, performed, improved, initiated, devised, designed, promoted, maintained, motivated, reorganized.

   Whatever you do, don't get too wordy. Be fascinating, but be short.
4. List only hobbies, avocations and interests which are pertinent to the job being sought.
5. You can have your resume professionally typeset and printed if you would care to, but most experts agree this will never be a factor in whether you are hired. Type it yourself or have somebody type it. Just make sure it is neat and that you have no errors, erasures or grammatical mistakes.
6. Follow this format:

   a) NAME, ADDRESS, PHONE (centered top-center).

   b) OBJECTIVE: If you are speculating with your marketing materials, you must make it clear to every employer what you are looking for. If this is the case be sure to include a description of the job you are seeking.

   c) EXPERIENCE: List each job, your title, then name and location, your duties, and how you used your skills. List most current job first, listing dates for each employer in left-hand column. How far back you go in time is determined by the pertinence of former jobs in relation to the one you are seeking. Use action words to describe your accomplishments. Be sure to list your reason for leaving each job.

   d) EDUCATION: If you have a college degree, spell it out and omit high school. If no post-secondary education, list high school. You might also list other courses, training, etc., if specifically relative to the job being sought.

   e) SKILLS: Go back to the list you made on page 17 and utilize all those skills that are now pertinent to the job you are seeking. List those applicable to the job.

f) COMMUNITY SERVICE, AWARDS, HONORS, ACHIEVEMENTS: As noted in Step One, jobs are often given to those who have similar interests to those of the employer or personnel manager. Don't be bashful, humble or modest in this category, even if it means going to a second page.

g) REFERENCES: Many books, articles, etc., on resumes will advise the applicant to simply state "Available On Request." We don't feel this should necessarily be so. It depends on your definition of references.

   Now we agree that names, addresses, and phone numbers of those persons who are willing to give you a good recommendation should not be included in the resume or sent with it. We feel that letters of reference, however, are an entirely different matter. They are selling tools, and as such, should definitely be sent with your resume and cover letter.

As an employer trying to weed out those to interview from those I couldn't bother with, I generally threw away those that didn't provide me with enough information to make a decision. Resumes always say what a person did on a job, but they sure don't give you a clue as to how well they did them. Even phone calls often don't divulge the true feelings of the former boss. He may be fearful of repercussions if he offers a negative opinion over the phone. Letters of reference, enthusiastically written, will often be the factor that gets you the interview.

HINT

Incidentally, if you worked for employers, did a good job, but left without getting a letter of reference, go back and get them now if you can. They are valuable and timeless.

Examples of resumes are shown on the next two pages.

STACEY AUSTIN
800 Main Street
Puma, Arizona 00000
(527) 777-7777

Objective:	Executive Secretary, with opportunity to advance to management and administration.
Experience:	
Feb. 1983 - Present	The Acme Company, 2072 Glendale, Phoenix, Arizona 00000, (527) 778-7788 Position: Executive Secretary Handle the business life of a very demanding vice-president and keep him in a good mood. Schedule appointments, transcribe and compose correspondence, monitor the requests to see him by phone and in person. Make all travel arrangements. Organize and implement staff and client meetings. Design and utilize money-saving forms and procedures. I am presently looking as there is no opportunity to advance in pay or position.
Aug. 1978 - Feb. 1983	Hot Acres Insurance Company, 123 Desert Flats Avenue, Torrid, Arizona 00000, (527) 725-3067 Position: Receptionist/Secretary Learned to act with speed, efficiency and presence of mind in this one woman office. Met everyone who entered and made them feel at home. Handled all phone calls and designated leads. Took shorthand from six agents and the owner. Typed all correspondence. Set appointments. Created and implemented computer programs. Organized new filing methods and procedures. Conceived and implemented a multiple calendar system for policy follow-up prior to dates of renewal. Kept everyone in a good mood and had fun doing it. Left as I was offered an executive secretarial job at higher pay.
July 1976 - Aug. 1978	Paupers Finance Company, 821 Distraught Avenue, Poverty Bend, Arizona 00000, (527) 826-4212 Position: Clerk/Typist/Collector Struggled with smiles and frowns while taking applications from new clients and trying to collect from delinquents. Extensive phone work, paper work and typing. Learned computer programming in night school to implement introduction of computer tracking of deliquency. Reorganized both collection and reception areas to accomplish confidential communication. My bosses felt duress was the only way to manage both employees and customers. I left to accept a position with a happy environment.
Education:	East Plateau Community College, Moccasin, Arizona Associate Degree in Secretarial Science, 1975 Tumbleweed Technical Institute, Mecca, Arizona Certificate: Computer Programming, 1976
Skills:	Type 70 wpm; shorthand 130 wpm, dictaphone, word processing, computer programming. Through practical experience I feel I also excel in human relations, organization and public speaking.
Community Service, Awards, Honors, Hobbies, Achievements:	Co-chairman of Puma City's 1983 Muscular Dystrophy Campaign. All State Puma High Women's Gymnastics. Kiwanis of Arizona 1980 Golden Throat Award for Public Speaking.
References:	Attached. Others on request.

JOHN M. ABLE
200 University Ave.
Ocala, Florida 33333
(305) 123-4567

Job Objective:	Entry-level Electronics Technician position, with opportunity to advance based on effort and efficiency.
Experience:	
1985 - Present (Part-time)	Joplin-Carey Co., Orlando, Florida Work 6 hour day while attending school. Maintain and install electronically controlled garage doors, both residential and industrial. Perform supervisory tasks when called upon. I am presently seeking a full-time position to better utilize my education. Although I like my present employer, additional hours and the opportunity to advance cannot be realized.
1982 - 1985	Acme Manufacturing Inc., Ocala, Florida Employed as one of 4 Maintenance Trouble-Shooters assigned to repair and maintain electronically powered machines. Enjoyed association with knowledgeable and experienced superiors. Received numerous commendations for punctuality, attendance, cooperation and desire, but realized I needed schooling. Management encouraged technical education and asked that I return. The Corp. moved out of state in 1986.
Education:	Macho Technical Institute, Frostproof, Florida
1985 - 1987	Earned Associates Degree, Electronic Technology, January 1987
Skills:	Particularly adept at blueprint and schematic reading and design, automobile electrical systems, and machine malfunction diagnosis.
Community Service, Awards, Honors, Hobbies, Achievements:	Assist annually with Florida Special Olympics. Black Belt in karate. Received Perfect Attendance Award upon graduation from Macho Tech. Member of Hamm Radio Operators of America. Enjoy golf, classical music, gymnastics, and experimenting with electronics in my home workshop. Climbed Mt. Everest in 1982.
References:	Letters of reference enclosed. Others on request.

OK. It's time to draft your resume. Do so below.

OBJECTIVE: ______________________________

____

EXPERIENCE: ______________________________

____

____

____

____

____

EDUCATION: ______________________________

____

____

____

____

____

SKILLS: ______________________________

____

____

____

____

____

COMMUNITY SERVICE, AWARDS, HONORS and ACHIEVEMENTS: ______________________________

____

____

____

____

____

REFERENCES: ATTACHED. OTHERS ON REQUEST.

LETTERS, ARTICLES, AWARDS — ATTESTING TO YOUR CHARACTER, INTEGRITY, PERSONALITY, ETC.

Anything you can fit in a copy machine that is significant as a tribute to your skills, attitude, character or personality is a marketing tool. Send them along with your references from former employers.

You may even have listed these things on your resume under COMMUNITY SERVICE, AWARDS, HONORS and ACHIEVEMENTS. That's OK. You are simply offering proof.

Items you may consider, which you may have forgotten:

a) Attendance awards from school
b) Write-ups on you — newspapers, school yearbooks, company newsletters, etc.
c) Paper awards — from charitable organizations for service rendered
d) Awards for sales, public speaking, writing, art, spelling or other skills

Make your own list. ____

____

____

____

____

____

____

____

____

____

____

____

____

____

Of the items you have listed, you have to be the judge of their value in relation to the job being sought. If you feel they attest to some attribute which may be desirable or of interest to the employer, then send them. If you have any doubts — don't.

You may be proud of the fact you were on the 6th grade soccer team which won the community championship, but it may not say much about you that's relevant to the job you are seeking. In fact, if an employer were to receive something that is truly insignificant, it may cost you an interview. Use good judgment.

After you have compiled all these materials, it is time to use them.

CHAPTER 8

TURNING LEADS INTO APPOINTMENTS

First of all, if you have taken our suggestion to work 40 hours or more a week on your "Ideal Job" hunt, then you are going to have a heavy schedule of things to do each day. So it is time to start using your "Things I Must Do Today" pages.

If you jam each page full of nine-to-five effort, we believe you won't need more than 30 pages. If you do, however, just make additional copies and keep them in your loose-leaf binder.

Get out a calendar now and write in the day of the week and the date on the top line of these forms. Keep going until you have a date written for the next 30 working days.

Under "Things I Must Do Today," start projecting your work. Leave the top portion of these forms blank for now. The telephone follow-up is only to be used for those you have already contacted.

1. Go back to page 27 and 28 of Chapter 5 and bring forward the names of all the employment agencies you are going to contact. Schedule each of them on the page of your choosing.
2. Go back to page 29 of Chapter 5 and project the date you intend to contact your state employment service on the calendar page of your choosing.
3. Go back to page 30 of Chapter 5 and project the date you intend to contact the Federal Job Information Center nearest your home on the calendar page of your choosing.
4. Now take the pertinent information from each "Prospective Employer Information" form and record it on the calendar page when you intend to follow-up. It is a good idea to schedule working on those employers who have run ads, or whom you have otherwise determined to be hiring now, before contacting employers where hiring is just speculative.

A specific written plan for each day is absolutely essential.

Each night before retiring, take the page for the next day and add to the items you have already written down. Fill each day with doing.

As you work your daily plan, check off each item after accomplishing it.

Incidentally, as you work your plan, you are going to become well acquainted with a copy machine in your area. Compare price, but don't sacrifice quality. Poor copies of anything should never be sent.

ENOUGH TALK. LET'S GET SOMETHING IN THE MAIL!

Working with your calendar for today and the "Prospective Employer Information and Follow-Up" forms, start sending your marketing materials. Then:

1. Record the date you sent the materials, in the follow-up section.
2. Record the date when you say in your cover letter you will be calling, in the follow-up section.
3. Record the date you will call, on the appropriate calendar page.
4. Make the calls assigned for today and record the outcome on the "Prospective Employer Information and Follow-Up" forms.

When making your follow-up phone call, don't forget to use the telephone technique outlined on page 33.

LET'S ASSUME YOU DO GET PUT THROUGH TO THE HIRING OFFICIAL, WHAT DO YOU SAY?

Much the same thing as you said in your cover letter, but only after you inquire if they received "the materials I sent." If they acknowledge receipt and that they were read, then ask for the interview.

Fill your voice with enthusiasm and a smile and yet be persistent. That old standby excuse, "We don't need anybody right now," just isn't valid and can be overcome.

"Yes, I realize that, but wouldn't it be nice to have one of the greatest workers in the world waiting in the wings the next time you do have an opening?"

As a salesperson selling this amazing product (you), you must realize that a potential sale is always possible until someone hangs up. Don't let it be you.

HINT

If you are working your "Ideal Job" hunt plan as you should, you are going to be away from home a great deal. This means you could easily miss that "once in a lifetime" phone call. Don't take this chance if there isn't someone always home to answer. Invest in a phone answering machine. And if you do, don't be clever or funny with the message you record. Play it straight!

CHAPTER 9

PREPARING FOR THE INTERVIEW

Again, let's talk attitude. Did you go on your last job interview hoping to get lucky, or full of self-confidence? Would you perhaps describe yourself as a nervous wreck? If so, let's change that feeling. Like public speaking, many of the butterflies will vanish if you know your subject well. Preparation for the job interview is vital as it affords you an edge over your competition. Most people will simply call on an ad, set up an interview and show up. No research, no thought of solving the employer's problems, no knowledge of the science of how to get hired.

That's why the candidates who get hired are not necessarily the best skilled or the most qualified. They often are, however, the most adept at selling themselves in the interview.

Over the years, I have made it a habit, when interviewing, to ask this question: "If today I were to interview 10 people, all of whom have the identical credentials on paper as you have, why should I hire you?" Fully 90% have sat there staring, not speaking — then shrugging their shoulders weakly muttered, "I don't know!"

As an employer who needed help, and was anxious to hire, I often exclaimed to myself, "For God's sake girl (or guy) — give me some reason to hire you!" Seldom did it come.

The average job candidate is so ill-prepared that no thought at all has been given to the fact that the employer ran the help-wanted ad in order to solve one of his problems. So when asked why he wants this job the ill-prepared candidate ignores the response the employer wants to hear, "I will enjoy solving your problem" — and says the stupid over-worked, self-defeating statement, "'Cause I need the money".

From now on, let's forget about what you need or want, until the employer shows an interest in you. Only then are you in a bargaining position.

If you successfully convince a prospective employer that you indeed are the means to solve his problem and help make him or his company more money he won't let you out of his office. He'll hire you on the spot.

So don't take this step in your "Ideal Job" hunt lightly. Know how to respond to any question. Don't be phony, however. You must fully intend to back up every statement you make!

How you respond to the interviewers' questions is probably the single most important factor in landing a job. Sufficient time should be spent, therefore, on the anticipation of both questions and answers.

Following, here, is a list of concerns which every employer has. Now, he may not ask you about some of these, because he either assumes he knows the answer or for some reason overlooks the subject. We strongly suggest you make a statement anyway that would answer the question had he asked it.

USE THE STATEMENTS YOU PREPARED ON PAGES 16, 17 AND 18 TO COMPLETE THE ANSWERS BELOW:

A) HONEST.

Seldom will he simply ask, "Are you honest?" Consequently you must assure him you are. Either provide letters which indicate you can be trusted or make a statement to the effect, "You can be sure I will never steal your goods or your time, my conscience doesn't allow it". On the lines below, write a statement you feel comfortable with that will assure the employer you are honest!

____

____

____

B) RESPONSIBLE.

Every employer would like to know that you are the type of person who is going to be on the job every day and on time. Further,that when given a job to do you will complete it on time. You might say: "Mr. Jones, I feel I am a reliable person, so you won't have to wonder if I'm going to be on the job as required and finish tasks on time. Rest assured I'll be here!" On the lines below, write a statement in your own words to the effect you are a responsible person.

____

____

____

C) A PERSON WITH CHARACTER.

Usually because of other employees he hired who are still with him or that he had to fire, the employer has fears that you have work flaws or character weaknesses. He may ask: "What are your major weaknesses?" In answering you try to get across that by no means are you perfect but that you are constantly striving to improve. For example: "I guess my greatest fault is impatience. Being an ambitious person who get things done, I resent people telling me, two or three times, that something must be completed. In the past, I have shown I was irritated. Now I just try to think — "take it easy, they don't realize yet how competent I am."" On the lines below, write a statement that would best describe your feelings, if asked this question.

____

____

____

D) A PERSON WHO IS NOT A CHRONIC COMPLAINER.

Chronic complainers are considered dangerous by most employers. They not only destroy morale but productivity along with it. Your prospective employer will be glad to hear you say something to the effect you are not a complainer. This is another area of employer concern that generally isn't put to the applicant in question form as who would admit that they complain? No one. It is often true that the complainer is blind to the fact he is a negative thinker and if asked if he were a chronic complainer would say, "Who, me? Of course not!"

A statement such as follows might put you in good stead with the employer. "I have always tried to be a positive thinker, so I don't like being around people who constantly complain. I always think that if there is something to complain about, then it is a challenge to my ingenuity to change it!" On the lines below, write a statement that you would feel comfortable with that will indicate to an employer that you are not the type of person who complains.

E) A PERSON WHO CAN FOLLOW DIRECTIONS.

There is an old saying that states, "There are two kinds of people who never go anywhere. Those who can't follow directions and those who can do nothing but."

So there are employees who wouldn't vacate a burning building unless told to do so, and then others that vacate any time the boss has his back turned. Some people feel they can do anything they want, when they want to, and how they want to, despite regulations to the contrary. They are "ulcer causers" yet every business seems to have one or two.

It's a good idea to let your prospective employer know you can follow directions. For example: "I see myself as a creative person but please know that creativity to me is not choosing my own paths to walk on. I believe in following directions, procedures and regulations. They are the means by which efficiency is standardized." On the following lines, write a statement in your own words which would indicate to an employer that you can follow directions.

F) A PERSON WHO PUTS COMPANY BUSINESS FIRST — BEFORE PERSONAL DESIRES.

Many employees, very frankly, take little interest in company growth, the quality of the product or service, overall morale, personal production or corporate profits. These same people are the first to complain, however, if hours are cut because of slow business, or raises aren't up to expectations. They are self-centered individuals who could care less even though the boss had to hold a garage sale to meet last week's payroll.

Among these apathetic individuals is: the clock-watcher (when leaving — not arriving), those that say, "That's not my job," those who use the phone liberally to call out and, too, encourage their friends to call them, those that call in sick from the beach or the ball park, those who have the idea that their sub-par work is "good enuff", those that spend more time in the restroom than the average kidney patient, etc., etc.

Now, the question you are asked may be something like, "How do you think you can contribute to our company?" or "What kind of employee do you think you'll make?" Your answer, if you can back it up, might be:

"I'm the type of person that wants to know if my company is making a profit, for if the company isn't making money, my future here is in jeopardy. I intend to give 100% and I expect others to do the same. That's the only way to compete effectively." On the lines below, write a statement that you feel comfortable with, that indicates you'll be a good company person.

____

____

____

G) A PERSON WHO IS A PROBLEM SOLVER NOT A PROBLEM FINDER.

(See following page)

The question posed by an employer may be something simple like: "Tell me, why should I hire you?"

In answering, you must make yourself sound as though you can do things as an employee that the others won't do, or can't do. You might respond as follows: "Because I am a problem solver. I love a challenge and consequently I enjoy solving problems particularly when others view them as excuses not to perform. I'll find answers simply because I know there is a solution to every problem and I'll keep looking 'til I find it!" On the lines below, write out a statement that you are comfortable with which indicates you are a problem solver.

____

____

____

____

____

____

____

____

____

THE DIFFERENCE BETWEEN A PROBLEM FINDER AND A PROBLEM SOLVER

THE PROBLEM FINDER

Problem Finders are easy to find. They are everywhere. They look like everyone else, however, they are more readily identified by sound. They say such things as, "somebody should do something about that", or "the rules are stupid", or "my boss is a jerk". The tone of their voice is also denotable. They whine, they cry, they shout, and seldom if ever consider that they possibly could be the cause of the problem. As such, they live with self-sympathy and a vehemently defensive attitude. They are never wrong, consequently, they find it impossible to apologize. They can't wait to spread slander, love to belittle others, and can hardly let an hour go by without complaining about someone or something.

Generally speaking, you can locate them in jobs which require little thought, little creativity, little responsibility, and no leadership ability. That is, if you can find them working at all. They are despised by employers, and at best, tolerated by conscientious co-workers, family members and would-be friends.

Problem finders are negative thinkers and, as such, chronic pessimists. They are depressing to be around and as a result have few friends. Their smiles are few and far between. They can't seem to smell the roses along the way, and simply aren't capable of being happy. They live with selfish motives in a lonely world.

If you know such persons, befriend them, be honest, be frank. Make them aware of the benefits of change. It can occur. Thank God, IT CAN OCCUR.

THE PROBLEM SOLVER

These persons are ninety times more difficult to find than the Problem Finders, but are still easily recognized by sight and sound. They find smiling comes easy and they project an image of self-confidence. Their immediate response to any problem, whether personally involved or not, is "What can I do to find a solution?"

Problems to them aren't something to simply complain about, procrastinate with or ignore altogether. Problems are challenges, opportunities to prove one's value when solved. Problem Solvers realize that with each solution found they become more valuable as leaders, as benefactors and as masters of their own destinies. They are wise enough to know they, too, will make mistakes, but unhesitatingly proceed to make decisions until the correct one is made.

Problem Solvers are positive thinkers, and as such, eternal optimists. They understand the futility of complaints, criticism, slander and living in the past. They also understand the promise for fulfillment which comes with goal setting, imagination and persistence.

Problem Solvers are leaders and do-ers. Always active, never bored and forever looking for new horizons. As such, they are sought after by more intelligent employers and bask in the luxury of good fortune. They are respected, admired and capable of greater love as they can see the good in the worst of men.

If you know such persons, stay close, and emulate their actions. You will grow in greatness and never experience the pains of loneliness or poverty.

H) A PERSON WHO IS HEALTHY.

The average employer is skeptical about people who have health problems simply because they are apt to miss work frequently.

If you do have a health problem you must convey to your interviewer that by no means will it interfere with your attendance or your productivity. Stress your attendance at school or at previous jobs if it was good. Bring letters from any source you can to indicate your health does not affect your efficiency and punctuality.

In answer to questions about your health, you might say: "It is because of living with (name your ailment) that I have developed a strong sense of self-discipline. I am stubborn with myself when responsibility is expected. I think you'll find I will not only be here but produce more than others."

If you are in fine health, then simply say something like: "As I am blessed with great health there is no reason why I won't be here every day and do more than is expected of the average person." On the lines below, write your own statement which you can use when asked about your health.

____

____

____

I) A PERSON WITH PERSONALITY.

Most employers recognize the value of a happy environment. Just one sour-puss can cause dissension, cliques, slander, animosity, jealousy — you name it. It's a fact that unhappy people simply don't produce.

A person with charm and a good sense of humor will often get hired before a more experienced person who doesn't know how to crack a smile.

Be warm, be friendly, be relaxed, be yourself. Smile, laugh at the interviewer's jokes (if you can do so without forcing it).

Remember, to get hired the interviewer must like you. The more he likes you, the less he will stress the qualifications you are lacking.

Now, the interviewer isn't going to ask you if you have personality so there is no answer to be prepared; however, it's not a bad idea to write down a few one-liners that you might slip in if the opportunity arises.

____

____

____

____

____

OTHER QUESTIONS YOU MAY WELL BE ASKED!

1. WHY DO YOU WANT TO WORK HERE?

"Prior to this interview, I did a great deal of research on your company as well as many others. I chose your company because I'm convinced it is a place in which I can succeed. I feel I am well qualified to be productive now, but I'll be even better in a short time as I'm anxious to learn." Now write your own statement in answer to this question.

____

____

____

____

2. WHY DO YOU WANT TO CHANGE CAREERS?

"I feel that my prior experiences have prepared me well for what I consider a step up. To me, this new career is a challenge I have long wanted and anxiously await. I am absolutely excited about it." (Mention exactly what makes you excited.) Now write your own statement in answer to this question.

____

____

____

____

3. WHY WERE YOU OUT OF WORK FOR SUCH A LONG TIME?

"After leaving my last job, I decided to do a little self-examination and research. I finally looked at the career objectives which I felt I would, and could, do best. I simply didn't want to rush into another dead-end job. Then, of course, I researched companies I would care to work for. I guess that's why it has taken me some time to get here today." Now write your own statement in answer to this question.

____

____

____

____

4. WHY DO YOU FEEL YOU WILL STAY AT THIS JOB WHEN YOU HAVE JUMPED AROUND SO MUCH IN THE PAST?

"Well, I finally got smart, analyzed my skills and desires and researched employers. I am anxious to construct a life-long career. Up 'til now, I've just taken the first thing to come along without considering compatability. My job hopping days are over!" Now write your own statement in answer to this question.

5. HAVE YOU HAD ANY EXPERIENCE IN A SUPERVISORY CAPACITY?

If you've had none specifically as an employee, draw from your personal experience with groups and organizations. If this is a blank, too, simply say, "while in school I coordinated student study groups," or perhaps "I worked closely with management to assign duties and analyze performance. I believe I would do well as a supervisor as I can get people to do things without arousing resentment." Now write your own statement in answer to this question.

6. HAVE YOU READ ANY GOOD BOOKS LATELY?

This may seem like an innocent question, but it is significant. The interviewer wants to find out if you take an interest in business, the profession you seek, self-improvement, current events, management, etc., if you read at all, and if your reading habits are restricted to sensational fiction. It's a good idea to pick up some business books that are best sellers and read them so you can say something like, "I'm halfway through *Iacocca* and I also thought *In Search of Excellence* was done very well."

Write here the books you have read or intend to read before the interview and the subsequent response you will make in answer to this question.

7. Now, from your last interview, write down the questions you were asked which you felt uncomfortable with, then prepare answers.

HINT

Think before answering any question. Why is this question being asked? Try to understand what the interviewer is trying to divulge. Answers can often reveal things about you that are better left unsaid.

WHAT EMPLOYERS CANNOT ASK YOU!

The laws today are very specific as to what can be asked by an employer in an interview or on the application.

It is illegal to ask you:

1. Your sex, if you are single or married, if you live with anyone, if you've ever been divorced or separated, when your divorce will be final, etc.
2. If you have children, how many, how old, who cares for them, why don't you have them living with you, do you plan on having any more children, etc.
3. Physical information such as weight, height, physical and/or mental handicaps, etc. (unless specific health requirements are necessary for the job in question).
4. If you've ever been arrested, jailed or convicted of a crime (unless security clearance is a requirement for the job in question).
5. If in the military, what branch of the service you were in, or if you received an honorable discharge.

6. Any reference to age other than, "are you over 18?"
7. Do you own a home, rent, live in an apartment, etc.
8. Any questions pertaining to your religious beliefs.

HOW DO YOU RESPOND TO A QUESTION THAT IS ILLEGAL, KNOWING THAT TO REFUSE TO ANSWER MAY RULE YOU OUT OF CONSIDERATION FOR THE JOB?

Use common sense.

1. If you feel the interviewer has no ulterior motive than to find the best candidate and you don't feel an honest answer can hurt your chances of being hired, then ignore the fact the question is illegal and answer the question.

2. If you can see how an honest answer can hurt your chances, we suggest you turn the situation around and ask the interviewer tactfully, "Just out of curiosity, why would you ask me that?" It is not a good idea to simply remind the interviewer that "That question is not legal!"

   In doing so, you are telling this person "you are wrong" and, as nobody likes to be told they are wrong, you are talking yourself right out of a job. By finding out the reason the question is being asked, maybe you won't mind answering it at all.

   Let's explore this further by taking a hypothetical situation. The interviewer has been taught that he should never hire a person who is going through a divorce. "These people are often depressed, preoccupied so as to neglect their work, and prone to excessive absenteeism." So the question is asked, "Are you currently going through divorce proceedings?"

   You then respond, "Just out of curiosity why would you ask that question?" The response comes, "Oh, believe me, it is nothing personal. We just simply want to know if you are going to miss work, and/or be working at less than your ability as the result of concentrating on your personal problems."

   You then respond, "I assure you I will give 100% to this job if I am hired and by no means will I ever allow my personal problems to affect my work, whatever they may be. I intend to control my destiny!"

   What you have done is answer the concerns of the interviewer without directly answering the question.

3. If the interviewer persists in asking illegal questions and is obviously unreasonable then state, "I do not feel that the question is relevant to the requirements of the position." This answer could well cost you the job but then you are probably better off not working for someone who is overly concerned about your personal life.

YOU ONLY GET A SINGLE CHANCE TO MAKE A GOOD FIRST IMPRESSION.

Many applicants for employment are ruled out of consideration before they ever open their mouths or present their application. Appearance is vital to your success as it says a great deal about you. Psychologists have determined that 60% of the impression you leave with others is based on visual contact.

HOW SHOULD YOU DRESS

In a word, dress safely. That is to say business-like and with attire that will offend no one.

HINT

During your research, find out how the interviewer dresses and how much emphasis the company puts on "Proper business attire." See these people in person if you can, then dress as they dress.

Men should wear suits, a long sleeve light-colored shirt (white is always good), conservative tie, and long, dark socks. If you can afford to buy a new suit, dark blues and greys are your best bet!

Leave your sportcoat at home along with any jewelry which could be considered "too much." Avoid loud colors when you choose your tie and make sure the style is currently being worn.

Women: most experts agree that a dark-skirted suit and a light colored blouse is preferable for an interview. The jacket should be full cut, the skirt — just below the knee, the blouse — long sleeve. No pantsuits!

While many women feel that dresses should be worn as they should be able to stress their femininity, just do so with caution. By no means should you try to use sex to get a job. This will get you a prompt refusal nine times out of ten — and probably in a dilemma the other time.

Good advice for men and women is: go easy with jewelry, colognes and make-up. Save these for your social life. Finger nails clean, cut and/or polished. Shoes neat and/or polished.

Before going on the interview, go through the initial meeting of a prospective employer with a friend playing the role of the interviewer. Then ask:

How is my appearance? Is it business-like?

How does my hair look? Style? Color?

How is my posture while standing? While sitting?

How are my facial expressions? Do I appear friendly? How is my smile?

How is my eye contact?

How is my body language? Does my walk convey confidence? Do my gestures and mannerisms add interest? Are they, perhaps, annoying?

HOW IMPORTANT IS BODY LANGUAGE?

What you convey to another person, without saying a word, is often overlooked in the wisdom offered to those seeking a job. It shouldn't be!

As director of a number of schools, I have seen this factor overlooked by many students who, obviously, never gave it much thought.

As they neared graduation, they sought assistance from the School Placement Department. They showed up looking like they just got off the bus after a week at Camp Hiawatha; promptly slouched down in a chair, crossing their legs, then, leaning back with their hands folded in back of their necks said, "OK, what jobs do you have for me?"

The frequency of this attitude has always been alarming, and every time it becomes evident, which is almost every day, I think to myself that our entire educational system is negligent in not having at least thirty (30) days per school year devoted to the application of Common Sense.

If you expect anyone to assist you to get a job, whether a school placement person or a long lost aunt or uncle, you must make them feel you are worthy. That's the only way they are ever going to be able to be enthusiastic about selling you to others.

So, your image, in the eyes of the placement director or the obligated relative, must be as polished as the one you present in an interview.

With body language, you can say a great deal. You can show respect, confidence, warmth, sense of humor, poise and interest. However, your body language will also show you lack any or all of the above. Be careful.

To this day, I recall one young lady who unsold herself in one fraction of a second. She was bright, attractive and had personality plus. She knew how to dress and, with her razor sharp wit, had come through the interview with colors flying. Then, the interviewer later told us, "when I was ready to say, 'can you start tomorrow,' she did something that turned me off completely, and I simply couldn't consider her after that." What could she possibly have done that was so terrible that she, instantaneously, killed the interview? She winked!

Every body movement tells a story. If you slouch — you're lazy. If you walk deliberately — you're too slow. If you seem to rush — you're too impulsive. If you're too fidgety — you're too nervous.

Ask friends to assist you. Practice in front of a mirror until you believe you are conveying the message with your body that is right for the job, and the image of the company where you expect to work. Incidentally, chewing gum is body language that will get you a fast rejection. Leave it at home.

HOW YOU SHOULD TALK

The other 40% of the first impression is what is heard. So, while what you say is of course vitally important, how you say it is equally significant.

Continue with your mock interview. Have your friend ask you all the questions on pages 52 through 58. Then ask:

How is my voice projection? Do I sound self-assured?

How is my voice inflection? Do I speak too much in a monotone?

How is my enunciation? Can you clearly understand me?

Am I talking too fast or too slow?

How is my expression? Do I sound warm, friendly, interesting, enthusiastic?

Do I sound knowledgeable?

Am I talking too much? Did I appear to listen well?

This last question is worth dwelling on for a minute or two. Over the span of far too many years, I have interviewed countless applicants who rated an A in every aspect of the interview except one. They simply didn't know how to listen. They were so intent on telling their story, that even when I did manage to slip in a word or two, they made it clear they didn't hear a thing. They went right back to what they obviously felt obligated to spit out without so much as a comment or reaction to my statement. Naturally, I didn't hire them. I also didn't tell them why I didn't hire them and, in retrospect, I suppose I should have. They are probably still out there somewhere pounding the pavement, wondering why employers don't listen to them. If some dear friend hasn't told them to SHUT UP, then I sincerely hope they get a copy of this book.

BE A GOOD LISTENER, PARTICULARLY IF YOU KNOW LITTLE ABOUT THE SUBJECT BEING DISCUSSED.

Some years ago, as head of my own advertising agency, I arranged for lunch at a plush club with two potential clients who had never met before. From a little prior investigation, I had learned that both had more than a casual interest in airplanes. As a matter of fact, both were alledgedly familiar with everything that had left the ground since Kitty Hawk. I sat there for better than an hour and a half, after the initial introduction, saying no more than an occasional "amazing" or "that sure is fascinating". These two men had the time of their life, and I am sure they could have cared less if I said a word or not. Each took turns parading their knowledge with great pride. As we were leaving, one of them turned to me and said, "you sure don't say much". I simply said, "That's because I know as much about airplanes as I do about women". I got both accounts.

THE PSYCHOLOGY OF TOUCHING

Two psychologists from the University of California at Riverside, Ronald E. Riggio, Ph.D., and Howard Friedman, Ph.D., in a study of those students identified as charismatic, determined that they physically touched people, while greeting strangers, far more often than others.

A study of the habits of waiters and waitresses, conducted by professors at Rhodes College in Memphis, Tennessee, also turned up some very interesting statistics. Tips actually doubled when these waitpersons made a point of physically touching their customers at some point in serving them.

The way you shake hands when starting and ending the interview is important. It says much about you.

Look directly into the person's eyes you are meeting and shake hands firmly.

Don't shake hands in the following manner:

1) The Ring Squeezer or Bone Crusher: Take it easy. No one likes a person who tries to impress someone with strength. This type of handshake is immediately resented and it is an indication to the experienced interviewer that you probably are trying to cover up an inferiority complex.

2) The Fish Hand: The limp hand is a surefire tip off that you lack confidence.

3) The Hand Pumper: The person who keeps pumping your hand up and down is usually insecure. The interviewer interprets this as a phony act. These people are usually trying to fake enthusiasm that they don't sincerely feel.

4) The Glue Hand: Nothing is more annoying than having someone hold your hand for a minute or so while they start conversation. They are also usually insecure.

5) The Hand Jerker: Those who give your hand one short "jerk" and abruptly withdraw their own are generally interpreted as people who don't really care to meet people. They have the attitude, "Okay, if we have to meet, let's get this over with in a hurry."

ABOUT TESTS

Many employers today use tests to qualify prospects for specific positions. Having spent years working with a variety of them, while acting as a consultant, I am a believer in their validity. Certainly not all of them, but many.

Most tests are not to be feared as they determine if a candidate is intellectually and emotionally capable of handling those duties which are to be performed. This being the case, the applicant is also served, as it is of little benefit to secure a job if, a few weeks later, frustration, stress and unhappiness occur as the result of incompatibility.

Tests can determine both under-qualification and over-qualification. Let me give you an example. If I want to hire a filing clerk, I want to find someone in the lower levels of mental alertness, but high in scanning accuracy; someone who is low in nervous tension (calm) and who is motivated by a need for security. Why? Those with a high degree of mental alertness would be almost immediately bored with the repetitive act of filing. Those with low scanning accuracy (which even a very bright person can be subject to) will make too many mistakes. A restless person simply can't adjust to staying in one place. Lastly, a person who is not highly motivated by security will not stay with the job and the company.

In taking these tests can you appear to be something you are not? As far as tests measuring mental alertness or acquired knowledge, no. As far as tests that measure aptitude and personality dimensions, yes. But be careful. Conflicting answers can often invalidate a test. It is best to be honest.

Realizing what the employer wants in a person, however, can sometimes be a clue as to how to answer. For example: let's say an employer wants to hire an outside salesman. Research has shown that those who perform best in this capacity have six distinct, but common characteristics. They are above average in mental alertness; they are more restless than calm; they are more gregarious than most; they are more assertive than the average person; they are competitive by nature; and they are motivated by the need for recognition more so than the average person.

Now, as a candidate for an outside sales job, you probably aren't aware of all these things, but you are pretty sure that a good salesman should be assertive rather than submissive. Therefore, when asked the question: If you were sitting in a partially filled theater and a big, mean, tough-looking guy came and sat in front of you and didn't bother to remove his hat, would you: A. Try to look around him? B. Ask him to remove his hat? C. Move to another seat? You should answer B.

Get the idea? Associate your answer with the actions you believe would be an asset on the job.

SOME OTHER IDEAS ABOUT TAKING TESTS

1. Don't panic when told you are going to be tested. Showing or commenting that you are upset may be more damaging than the test results.
2. Even if being timed, make sure what you are able to do is correct. You'll get no positive results by rushing to put down an answer to all the questions if they are all wrong. It's better to indicate you are a little slow but accurate, than fast and stupid.
3. Don't overcompensate for your anxiety by trying to be too calm. A certain amount of stress is a good thing. It is normal and it makes us perform.
4. Make sure you have some scrap paper in your pocket to use with math questions. Generally this is permissable, but many times the person administering the test won't provide it.
5. Read all instructions thoroughly. If there is anything you don't clearly understand, ask for clarification before starting.

ABOUT PAPER AND PENCIL HONESTY TESTS

There are many honesty tests on the market. A few of them are very good. As a matter of fact, they are about as reliable as the polygraph. Unlike the polygraph, however, which has been deemed illegal in most states, the paper tests have been cleared as non-discriminatory in many courts and are legal.

Now, you might think, as these tests simply acknowledge what the applicant admits, that they can't be effective. Not so! They work because those taking the test believe their morals reflect those of society at large. They feel as though they can't appear too honest as people will think they are not honest. Ponder this for a while — you'll understand.

One other supposition goes into the evaluation of these tests. The creators believe "once a thief, always a thief." So any admission of past guilt is an indication you will probably steal again.

If you now feel proud of your reputation for honesty and integrity, and that reputation has been earned, may I suggest you refrain from admitting your past sins. You could well be refused a job for reasons which now are not factual. These tests are good, but they are far from being infallible.

THE EMPLOYMENT APPLICATION

If during your research of a company, you make a personal visit, make it a point to pick up an application for employment. Even if you call the company, ask if they will send you an application. If you, subsequently, do get an interview with that company you will appear much more professional when you show up with an application that is filled out in its entirety, neatly done, and with no errors. This is particularly important if your handwriting looks like the average doctor's prescription. You will have an opportunity to type it.

Over the years, I have had numerous applicants ask to borrow a phone book to look up addresses and numbers. In so doing, they convinced me that they didn't have it "all together." You must think ahead if you expect to present a favorable image.

If you can't get a company employment application, then go to an office supply store and get a standard form. Fill it out completely and have it with you when you go on an interview. You can then copy the information on the company's application with the assurance that it is correct.

CHAPTER 10

INTERVIEW PREPARATION CHECKLIST

A chain is only as strong as its weakest link. Your plan to get hired is similar. Just one weak aspect can overshadow all your strong points. One inadvertent slip-of-the-tongue and you've blown it! One admission of ignorance and it's "back to the drawing board." One "I don't know" and it's return to square one time.

Be ready or stay home!

The entire purpose of the step-by-step procedure is to make sure you are organized — more organized than any of your competition. If you have followed directions, you undoubtedly are, but as a final act before leaving for the interview, let's make sure.

Go over the following checklist. Make a "✓" in the boxes in the right-hand column only when you are 100% confident.

1. I know how to dress and have picked out the clothes I know will be viewed as acceptable . . . ☐
2. I know the means of transportation I am going to use to get to the interview . . . ☐
3. If I am driving a car, I know it is running well and I have checked the tires, the oil and the gas . . . ☐
4. I know the route I am going to travel and I know what time I must leave in order to get there, at least, fifteen (15) minutes early . . . ☐
5. I know where I can park and I have money to park . . . ☐
6. I know the name of the receptionist and/or the name of the secretary of the person who will conduct the interview . . . ☐
7. I know the name and correct title of the person(s) who will hold the interview, and I know a great deal about their personality and background . . . ☐
8. I know the name of the Department Head who will play a role in the hiring decision, and I have researched background and personality . . . ☐
9. I know who owns the company (names, titles, etc.). If a corporation, I know the names of the officers and the Board Members, and a few facts on all of them . . . ☐
10. I will take a briefcase or attache case with me to the interview, and I have it packed with: a) an application (already filled out), b) additional copies of my resume, c) samples of my work, d) additional letters of reference or communication, e) a notebook to record any dates, names, pertinent facts, etc., that I can use later in follow-up letters, and f) my purse (if a woman) . . . ☐
11. I know a great deal about the company, products or services, policies, procedures, profits, etc. . . . ☐
12. I have studied the questions I will most likely be asked and I am prepared to answer them . . . ☐

13. I feel I know the type of employee the average employer wants to hire and I have prepared statements which should answer their concerns . . . ☐

14. I know the signals which indicate the company may be interested in hiring me . . . ☐

15. I know the questions I intend to ask after the company has shown an interest in hiring me . . . ☐

16. I know to ask a question in return when asked a question that is illegal to ask, or one that I simply would prefer not to answer . . . ☐

17. I know the salary range and benefits I will ask for after the company has indicated a desire to hire me . . . ☐

18. I know the specific job I would like to have with this company, and I have studied the job description . . . ☐

19. I understand how to observe the interviewer's office to look for conversational clues . . . ☐

20. I know I am to speak up. I know what to say and what not to say. I know how to put expression in my voice. I know when to shut up and be a good listener . . . ☐

21. I know I am going to shake hands firmly while looking people in the eyes . . . ☐

22. I know the posture I want to use while standing, walking and sitting . . . ☐

23. I understand the value of using people's names, but I also know that, when addressing people in responsible positions, it is safe to address people as "Ms.," "Mrs.," or "Mister," regardless of age differences . . . ☐

24. I have prepared a few one liners to use if the opportunity presents itself . . . ☐

25. I know the closing statement I am going to use if I feel I really would like the job . . . ☐

26. I know the statement I am going to make if I'm not sure I want the job . . . ☐

27. I know how to reject an offer of employment without causing resentment . . . ☐

28. I realize I must be polite if rejected in the interview and act with class and distinction . . . ☐

29. If rejected in the interview, I am prepared to tactfully ask "why" by soliciting the help of the interviewer . . . ☐

30. I am mentally prepared to sell myself with enthusiasm. I am going to step in the door with a smile on my face, and everyone I meet is going to like me . . . ☐

I AM READY!!! ☐

CHAPTER 11

THE INTERVIEW

When you arrive for your appointment, ten to fifteen minutes early, go right to work. Greet the receptionist and/or secretary by name and thank them for being so cordial on the phone when you called earlier. Do this, even if you actually felt they were a little cold over the phone, for chances are you will also be calling them again after the interview.

You must always be thinking, "how can I set myself apart from the other candidates?"

The time arrives — "Mr. Brown will see you now!" That's when you put your enthusiasm in high gear. After a warm greeting and a firm handshake, you sit down, but while doing so, look around the room for further clues about this man.

Is the office elaborate or just functional, expensively decorated or very practically done? Are there any plaques, diplomas, awards, trophies? Are there any photographs of famous people, or ones denoting he or she is a fisherman, a hunter, a golfer, a tennis nut, etc.? Are there family pictures on the desk, books, or any items that might designate a hobby, avocation, collection?

Simply put: be observant! Every personal item in an office is a key to conversation. You may find out that you have things in common that will turn out to be a great plus.

My son-in-law recently went on a job interview and noticed a family photo taken with a school building in the background that looked familiar. As it turned out, he had hit a home run through this man's bedroom window about twelve years earlier. The interviewer asked, "That was you?" Then, they both laughed uproariously as they recalled the incident.

Enthusiasm sells. If you show you are the person who most wants this job, you've got a great chance of getting it! Remember, though, you want this job because you feel you will love it and will do a sensational job. Keep money out of the conversation until the time is right.

A Detroit businessman, now known by everyone in town as Mr. Belvedere, rose from obscurity to great wealth selling home improvements. His marketing secret was simple, yet astoundingly successful. He ran TV commercials describing various jobs, then, turned to the camera at the close and emphatically, and believably, stated, "we do good work." He paused after each word and said each with feeling — and the phone rang off the hook.

If you were to use the same technique and emphatically state, "I want this job," you stand an excellent chance of being taken seriously.

WHAT IS BETTER OFF LEFT UNSAID

Don't make the mistake of slandering anyone. Remember what Mom said, "If you can't say something nice about someone, don't say anything at all." Particularly stay away from discussing your family, your acquaintances, former employers and former bosses, unless in a very positive manner. Avoid politics, religion and sports altogether, unless you are certain of the interviewer's feelings. It simply is not wise to offer a contradictory opinion on any subject.

AVOID STATEMENTS THAT CAN GET YOU IN TROUBLE

Some years ago, I advertised to fill two vacancies on the same day. I needed a maintenance man and a student counselor. I had over a hundred calls for the counseling job but only one response for the maintenance position. I don't think I'll ever forget him.

I was seated in my office in the middle of a meeting with an important government official, when this fellow poked his head in the door and without so much as an "excuse me" said, "Hey, are you the guy I see about the janitor job?" Now, I instantaneously thought, "What a jerk!" but as I needed a man and he was the only one that inquired, I would withhold judgment. I said, "Please see the girl at the counter to your right and fill out an application." He mumbled something about being in a hurry but did get the application.

I concluded my meeting and asked the man to step into my office. He looked as though his electric razor was in the pawn shop and his clothes were "early depression." I glanced at his application and, to my surprise, I saw a friend of mine listed as a reference — a very prominent attorney with whom I had gone to high school. I impetuously asked, "How do you know Emmett Baystrom?" He, just as impetuously, answered, "Oh, Emmett baby — he's my man — my attorney. On my last job, I got in an argument with my boss and I killed him, and Emmett got me off free as a bird."

After my tongue returned to the position in the mouth necessary to utter sounds, I said, "Well, thanks very much for coming in. We'll be interviewing applicants all this week before making a decision, and we'll give your application ample consideration."

This story is absolutely true. I have often thought that had this applicant not volunteered this information and, instead, said, "Mr. Baystrom and I worked together on a case he was involved in," — I might have hired him. It has occurred to me, too, that I might also have needed an authentic ghostwriter to assemble this book.

If you want to get hired, watch what you say, rely on prepared statements, and don't volunteer information that could possibly portray you as a potential problem.

DON'T BE A SNOB OR A BROWN-NOSER

Phony compliments, putting on airs and name-dropping are all excellent ways of blowing an interview. Be sincere and sell yourself with humility. If the interviewer mentions he is proud of his 160 bowling average, you may have a great anxiety growing inside of you to tell him you average 180 — but fight the tendency. Say nothing, and simply respond, "That's very good!" If he asks if you bowl and what your average is, you, of course, can say so, but add, "I think the lanes I bowl at must be easy, as I ordinarily am not that good."

ABOUT SMOKING

As a general rule, don't smoke, either while waiting for the interview or in the interview. Play it safe. Many people are very biased about those who use cigarettes, cigars or pipes.

Therefore, you won't score any points by asking, "Do you mind if I smoke?" Keep your mouth shut. If the interviewer lights up a cigarette, then go ahead, but if you have no idea if the interviewer smokes, don't light up and don't ask.

If you are asked, "Do you smoke?" don't lie if you do. Just say, "I've been seriously trying to quit."

SELL THE INTERVIEWER ON WHAT YOU CAN OFFER BEFORE YOU EVEN START THINKING ABOUT WHAT THE EMPLOYER CAN DO FOR YOU.

Over the years, I have had many applicants start off the interview by asking what the position pays. In so doing, they promptly designed an early exit for themselves.

Can you imagine a salesperson walking into a prospect's office and saying, "What will you pay for a typewriter?" "I have one here for sale." Well, if this were the last typewriter in the world and typewriters were all identical in function, he/she might get a positive response. Otherwise, the prospect would think you are crazy.

Selling yourself in an interview is no different than selling a product. You must offer benefits to create interest and desire before discussing price. To do this, use the statements you prepared in Step Seven. Then, be a good listener. Answer the interviewer's questions, then, look for clues that indicate the interviewer has an interest in hiring you. If he doesn't, then asking for a particular wage is a moot point.

HOW CAN YOU TELL YOU HAVE SOLD YOURSELF WELL?

1. When the interviewer says, "You remind me of myself."
2. When he calls other people in the company to step in his office to meet you.
3. When he starts selling his company as hard as you sold yourself.
4. When the interviewer shows he is comfortable talking to you.
5. When he gives you a tour of the company, introducing you to people as you progress.
6. When the interview lasts more than thirty minutes.
7. When he asks, "When would you be available to start work?"
8. When he goes into great detail explaining the fringe benefits of the company.
9. When he asks, "What kind of a starting wage are you looking for?"
10. When he starts talking about positions you can advance to after you have been with the company awhile.

WHEN YOU ARE SURE THE COMPANY IS INTERESTED IN YOU, ASK YOUR QUESTIONS. ONLY THEN ARE YOU IN A BARGAINING POSITION!

You might preface your questions by saying, "I'd like to make sure this is the job I'm going to throw my heart and soul into, so if it's OK with you, I'd like to ask you a few questions."

Incidentally, by asking sound, intelligent, well thought out questions, you will enhance the probability of your hiring. A candidate who has no questions to ask conveys the idea that thinking is not one of his/her strong suits.

1. Has there been high turnover in this position?
2. Is the person who had this position last still with the company? If so, would it be possible for me to talk to him/her?
3. Are openings for the better positions generally filled from within?
4. If I do an exemplary job, when might I expect to be promoted?
5. Are there problems with this position which need solving?
6. Is there a written job description for this job that I might take a look at? (Only if you have not already obtained one.)
7. What is the average work week of the person filling this position?
8. What does the future of this company look like to you?
9. Do you feel that most of the employees who work here enjoy coming in each day?
10. Is there any chance I will be asked to relocate or travel?
11. Will I be responsible to answer to just one person, or will I have a multitude of bosses?
12. Are there any serious problems the company is experiencing now?
13. Is there any probability the company will be sold?
14. Do you have any questions or concerns about my ability to do this job?
15. When do you expect to make a hiring decision relevant to this position?

If you have other questions you want to ask — record them here ____________________

CLOSING THE INTERVIEW

Like closing a sale, any good salesperson knows you must ask for the order. In this case, you must ask for the job.

A sharp interviewer knows that a person who shows he really wants the job will most probably be a better employee. If you have concluded that "this is the job for me," then, by all means, say so with conviction.

Here are a few examples:

a) Thank you for the interview, Mr. Brown, I'm very impressed with both you and your company. I'd like to go to work here, and believe me, if given the chance, you will be proud of the job I do.

b) Mr. Brown, I am excited at the prospect of working here. Just say the word and I am ready to start. I'm confident you will be pleased with my work!

MAKE UP YOUR OWN STATEMENT HERE TO USE WHEN CLOSING AN INTERVIEW FOR THE JOB YOU WANT ____________________

____

____

____

WHAT IF, AFTER QUESTIONING, YOU ARE NOT SURE YOU WANT THIS JOB!

Simply go to a warm good-bye, after the interviewer details his final statement. Usually this will be a few words to tell you when a decision will be made. You might then respond:

"Thank you so much for your time, Mr. Brown; it has been a very enjoyable half hour."

WHAT IF YOU ARE OFFERED THE JOB ON THE SPOT, BUT YOU AREN'T SURE YOU WANT THE JOB?

Be courteous, warm and friendly while saying something like:

"Thank you, Mr. Brown, but if it is OK with you, I'd like to give this some very serious thought. I want to clearly feel I will be pleased with the company and have no doubts that I can do my best. May I get back to you on Thursday?"

WHAT IF YOU ARE REJECTED ON THE SPOT? WHAT DO YOU SAY?

If you are turned down for any job, you are going to feel disappointed, but try not to let your pride get in the way of common sense by showing anger and resentment. Be a good sport in defeat; leave the interview showing you have class. In so doing, that interviewer can still be a valuable ally. Perhaps he'll consider you for other positions. Perhaps he'll put in a good word for you at another company. Who knows? Life takes some funny turns. Alienating contacts along our path will never serve to benefit our search for security and happiness.

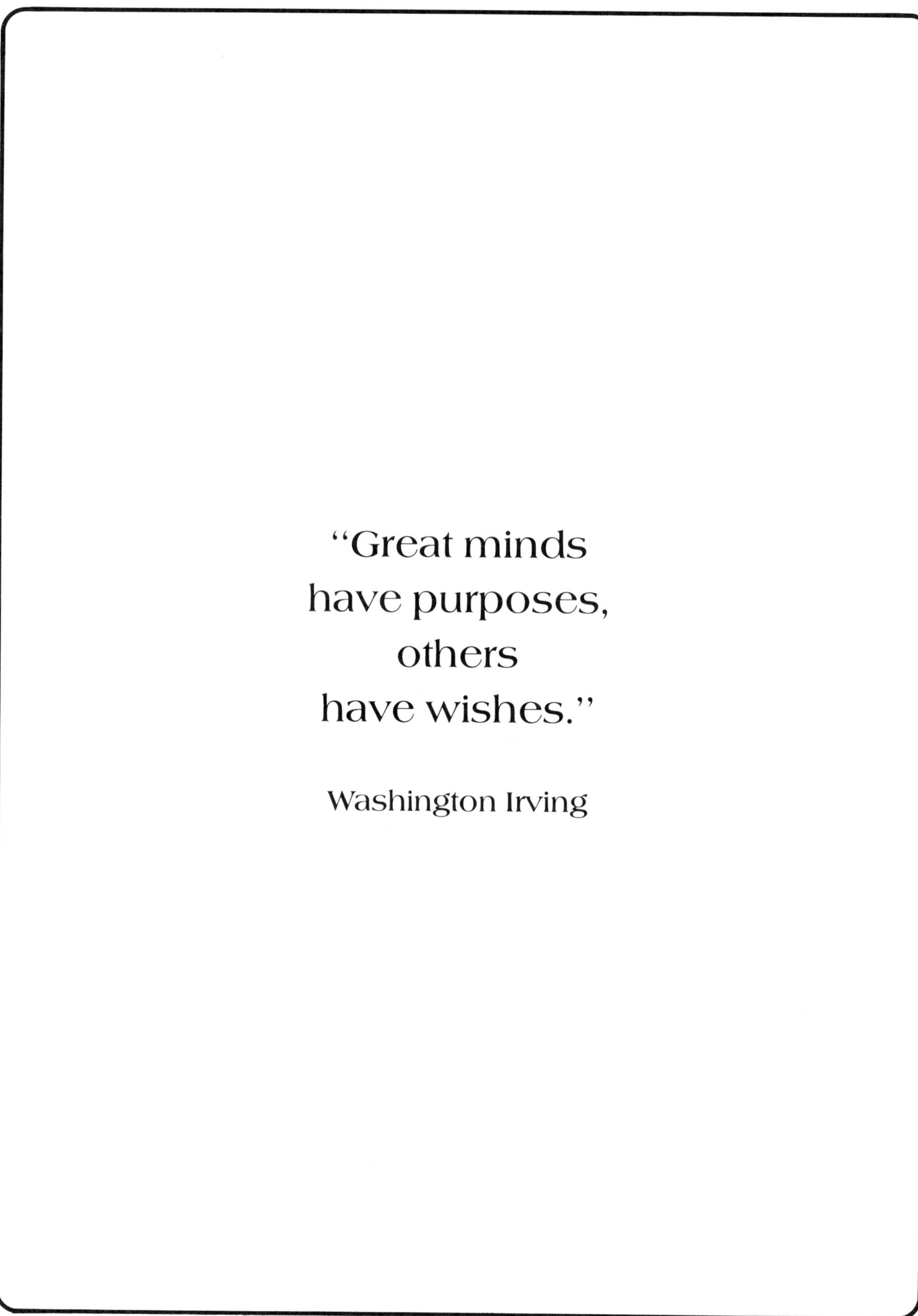

"Great minds
have purposes,
others
have wishes."

Washington Irving

CHAPTER 12

AFTER THE INTERVIEW

The employer said to the young man, "So, you want to go to work, do you?" The answer was quick and, unfortunately, honest. "No sir, I just really need a job!"

Over the years I have seen many people convey this idea, but, it seems, particularly by the young. Countless times I have heard the same response to the question, "Have you been able to find a job yet?" The answer, "Well, I've turned in at least 15 applications and now I'm just waiting for one of them to call." Wrong, wrong, wrong!

Every good salesman knows never to assume that a sale is made until the contract is signed. If he feels the sale is yet possible after leaving the prospect, he immediately takes steps to keep the prospect warm. He writes letters, sends articles of interest, calls to set up a luncheon, asks him to join him at the game, etc.

The formula for selling yourself into a job is quite similar. You must keep the possibility of hiring you on the front burner. You must separate yourself from the other prospects. Here are a few suggestions:

1. Send a letter immediately, thanking the employer or his agent for interviewing you. Reiterate your strong desire to work for the company and to work hard. State in your own words how you feel you can benefit the company — how hiring you can result in saving the company an expense or bringing in new revenues. State firmly that you are honest, responsible, considerate, skilled, industrious and compatible with others.
2. Send along any letters, awards, certificates, etc., which you did not have at the interview, that will attest to the virtues you mention in your letter.
3. Send articles or items which you know are of interest to the person who interviewed you. For example, if during the interview the interviewer mentioned that he is just starting to jog as he must get into better shape, you might just send an article on the subject. But, by no means, send a costly gift.

Several years ago, after waiting at length for his interview, a man finally got the chance to sell himself. He was ushered into the boss' office, shook hands and confidently began his introductory remarks. He was well prepared, but not for the unexpected. After a few brief questions, the boss announced that he'd have to cut the interview short as he had to leave to attend his twelve-year-old daughter's musical recital. She played the flute and, as the boss put it, "She is remarkable for her age!"

The man being interviewed was greatly disappointed but had the presence of mind not to show resentment. It was clear the boss's daughter was far more important to him than holding one more lengthy interview. After all, he had already been through six interviews that day. The applicant said, "Believe me, if it were my daughter who excelled at music, I would be there."

He then left the interview and went straight to the record store with which he dealt. He went through the stacks of records until he found a somewhat rare collection of pieces by flutist James Galway. He went home, wrapped it up, and promptly put it in the mail with the enclosed note:

> "It was a great pleasure meeting you today for it is rare to find a man who can equally share his love — with his family and with his business. Ironically, after leaving your office, I happened upon the record I have sent along. 'Just luck!' I thought your daughter might like it!"
>
> Respectfully Yours,

He got the job!

As stated earlier, jobs don't always go to the best qualified. Your ability to make the interviewer like you and want to hire you is most significant!

Now, as to your assignment. Don't attempt to write in this step until after an interview, but do so as soon as you can when you return from the interview, while the thoughts are clear in your mind.

What if you should determine in the interview that you don't care to work for this man or for this company. Should you write anyway? Yes, definitely! You have a reputation to live up to — an image that must be maintained. By writing to say, "Thanks, but no thanks," you depict yourself as a professional person. You never can tell, as time goes by, when that same person will have an opportunity to speak well of you.

Reputations are earned. Never neglect an opportunity to project a favorable image.

After the interview, draft a letter below. Using the ideas briefly spelled out on the previous page, break your letter into four paragraphs . . . .

Paragraph A) What you think of the company and the person who interviewed you, and why you want to work there.

Paragraph B) What you feel you can do for the company.

Paragraph C) The attributes you possess in character and personality which back up the statement of self-confidence you have made in paragraph B.

Paragraph D) What you have shown you can do based on experiences you have had that back up the statement of self-confidence you have made in paragraph B.

. . . Then, a warm close.

____

____

____

____

____

____

____

____

____

Okay, now that you have the letter done, write down all the additional documentation you intend to send with the letter which will help confirm the statements you made in the letter.

1.

2.

3.

4.

Finally, make notes on the Prospective Employer Information forms recording any interests the interviewer divulged during the course of the interview which would indicate he might appreciate receiving either articles or items. Then record on the top of the appropriate work-calendar page when you intend to follow up.

CONTINUE TO FOLLOW UP BY PHONE OR IN PERSON

Again, working with your prospect forms and your daily calendar sheets, make sure you follow up when you say you will follow up. Keep calling or visiting until a conclusion is final.

If you continue to get the answer "we haven't made a decision yet," then you can assume you haven't sold yourself as well as you might. You can also assume, however, that no other applicant has either or you would have been told in one way or another that you needn't bother to call again. What can you do to make this decision maker say okay?

THROW DOWN A CHALLENGE!

This method has worked successfully for many. It simply tells the employer you are very confident of your abilities and know if given the opportunity, you'll be great on the job.

"Mr. Jones, there are other employers I have anticipated working for, but, very frankly, you have sold me on your company. Let me work for you for two weeks at no pay so I can erase all doubts from your mind. If at the end of that time, I haven't completely sold you on the fact I'm the person for the job, just say so and I'll walk out of your life — no questions asked."

After saying this, just wait for an answer. Very often this expression of self-confidence will encourage the employer to hire you. Seldom, however, will you be asked to work at no pay!

EMPLOYMENT CONTRACTS

If you have been offered a position which is yet obscure in the detail of your duties, responsibilities, authority or remuneration it is to your advantage to get something in writing. This agreement should be signed by yourself and the owner or an officer of the corporation. Oral promises are worthless when the man doing the promising either leaves the company, or changes his mind and denies his promises as you claim them to be. Many such oral agreements have also turned to nothing less than complete frustration when companies changed management or ownership.

As the company has now indicated they want your services, you should be in a good position to get an employment contract. Don't simply ask the company to put it in writing, however, as this could result in producing a defiant attitude on the part of the employer.

I suggest you handle this situation in this manner: "What you have proposed sounds very fascinating, but so that we both are fully aware of all facets of the understanding between us, I would like to write down this agreement, as I see it, and present it to you for your approval. Is that acceptable to you? Any company with legitimate intentions should have no objections to this reasonable request. If they do object, then I suggest you think again about accepting the job.

A few years ago, I learned, too late, the values of having promises in print. I was recruited by a large corporation to take over a branch in California which was in trouble. This meant relocation, so I was very exact when clarifying the specific points of my authority. Those which, to me, were essential. At meetings in Chicago, and then California, I was assured that I could move items within my budget as long as gross expenditures did not exceed the total budgeted. Both times I received the response, "No problem".

Five months later, profits were measureably better, the branch was out of difficulty and projections for steady growth were excellent. I had given them what they wanted — solutions and stability. But I also gave them one other advantage, the time to find a replacement who would work for less. They reneged on their promises, and when confronted with the fact they lied to me, their answer was surprisingly honest: "Yes we did!" They were confident I couldn't prove a thing. They were right.

So take it from me. It is wise to have both parties in full agreement on all aspects of performance and wiser yet to have a contract signed by accountable individuals.

WHAT TO DO IF YOU ARE EXPERIENCING DELAYS IN FINDING YOUR "IDEAL JOB"

First of all, don't give up the hunt. If you are putting forth honest effort and working your plan, your persistence will eventually pay off.

Even if you have one foot in the "Poor House," don't give in to the urge to accept a second rate job. You can hold on if you put your ingenuity to work. Create a business for yourself. All you have to do is use the skills you now possess in an organized manner.

There is hardly any occupation which can't be marketed by an individual. Design your service on paper, then determine if you can reach your prospective customers best by newspaper ads, distributing flyers, personal visits, or by phone.

Anyone with a Degree can usually make money as a Consultant, Tutor, Research Analyst, Tax Preparer, or Bookkeeper, or with a variety of other business and educational services.

Specific vocational skills are even easier to market. There are many small businesses that would be pleased to find a person who performs clerical services at home. Typing and word processing can be excellent sources of income, particularly if you pick-up and deliver. If you are skilled in the use of computers, consider offering your talents as a trainer.

There are many homeowners who need the help of those who are skilled in any of the building trades, electronics, auto mechanics, appliance repair, heating and cooling, etc. All you have to do is to make people aware of the fact that you are available.

Those in the Health professions can make some reasonable sums by assisting with the care of the aged, the handicapped, or the infirmed who reside in private housing.

When looking for additional sources of income, don't fail to examine your avocations. Very often you can turn a hobby into big bucks. If you are a photographer, think about taking pictures at weddings. If you like to cook, how about catering? Love to dance? — teach it! Put on your thinking cap.

Whatever you decide to do, be thorough in your planning. Find out from others how they did it. Write everything down. Set up a budget. Know for sure you can make a profit. Keep accurate records. The IRS has little pity for the ignorant.

If you have the will power to elude the lazy habits that can preoccupy your time, you could end up with both your "Ideal Job" as well as an ongoing source of additional income which you also enjoy doing.

CHAPTER 13

12 WAYS TO PROMOTE YOURSELF AFTER FINDING YOUR "IDEAL JOB"

1. From your first day on, show up early. Never be late. Salaries go up as responsibility increases. Those who are chronically late, label themselves irresponsible. And, as such, not suited for supervisory positions.
2. Study the Science of Handling People. This skill, if soundly developed, will result in more advancement opportunities than any subject you have mastered in school. Start with buying a copy of Dale Carnegie's *HOW TO WIN FRIENDS AND INFLUENCE PEOPLE.* This book has been a best seller for many years and for good reason. We wholeheartedly recommend it.
3. From your first hour on the new job, write a training manual while you learn. Answer those questions that perplex you in print so that the person who replaces you will be able to adapt more quickly without the pain that accompanies trial and error. Show it to your supervisor when you have completed it.
4. Never turn in any report, project, letter, assignment, etc., which you have not checked over and over again for accuracy. From your day of arrival, fashion an image of thoroughness and professionalism.
5. Take the time necessary to dress as a person in management should dress. From the very start, sell the idea that you take pride in your appearance.
6. Maintain a smile and a positive attitude.
7. No matter what may occur, don't destroy yourself by complaining, or slandering others. Bite your tongue if you have to. Chronic nay-sayers simply don't get promotions. Leaders find solutions.
8. If you know something is not right, and you feel like criticizing, don't. It will serve you no purpose. Figure out an alternative that will effect a positive change, then present it. And, do so, void of the tendency to prove someone else wrong.
9. Never argue. Nobody ever wins an argument. Does this mean you shouldn't disagree? Of course not. If you have a mind of your own, you definitely will have differing opinions. When that time comes, however, stay calm. Don't raise your voice. Instead, bet a lunch or a cup of coffee. You'll prove you have management potential.
10. Look for opportunities to revise procedures, forms, methods, designs, etc., that if accomplished, will save the company time or money. Many times it is just accepting as a challenge what everybody else is complaining about.
11. Make a point of taking notes when conversing with management or when in meetings. You'll be noticed for doing so. Also keep a daily log of your accomplishments. If questioned on a particular point, you'll be able to state how, what, when and where. It is wise, too, to continue your practice of charting your "Things I Must Do Today" list.
12. Have a good word for everyone, . . . every day.

Your ideas, suggestions, comments, and experiences are welcome. If accepted for publication, you will receive a gift of appreciation. All contributions based on experiences must be factual and authenticated by others, if at all possible.

Send your materials to:

Editor
Progressive Publications
P.O. Box 4016
Homosassa Springs, Florida 32647

Press On

Nothing in the world can take the place of persistence. Talent will not; nothing is more common than unsuccessful men with talent. Genius will not; unrewarded genius is almost a proverb. Education alone will not; the world is full of educated derelicts. Persistence and determination alone are omnipotent.